D0236223

Cracking ANTIQUES

Cracking ANTIQUES

KATHRYN RAYWARD & MARK HILL

MITCHELL BEAZLEY

Picture Credits

The Publishers would like to thank the following for the use of images in this book. **Auction houses, antiques dealers and collectors:** Antique Glass @ Frank Dux Antiques, Bath; Art Deco Etc, Brighton, East Sussex; Ashmore and Burgess; Dr Graham Cooley; Design 20C, Surrey; The Design Gallery, Westerham, Kent; Dreweatt's, Donnington, Berkshire; End of History, New York; Festival for Midwinter, London; Fieldings, Stourbridge; Freeman's, Philadephia, PA; Richard Gardener Antiques, Petworth, Sussex; TW Gaze, Diss, Norfolk; The Glass Merchant, Surrey; Gorringes, Lewes, East Sussex; Adrian Grater, London; Michelle Guzy, Stafford, Staffordshire; Jeanette Hayhurst, London; John Howard @ Heritage, Woodstock, Oxon; KCS Ceramics, Feltham, Middlesex; Lyon & Turnbull, Edinburgh; Mallets, London; Manic Attic, London; Galerie Maurer, Munich; R&G McPherson, London; Pook & Pook, Downingtown, PA; Quittenbaum, Munich; Rago Arts & Auction Center, Lambertville, NJ; Rosebery's, London; Rossini, Paris; Skinner Inc, Boston, MA; Sollo:Rago Auctions, Lambertville, NJ; Swann Galleries Image Library, New York; Kerry Taylor Auctions, London; Tennants, Leyburn, N Yorkshire; Titus Omega, London; Toronto Antiques Center, Toronto; Galerie Vandermeersch, Paris; Vetro & Arte Gallery, Venice; Woolley & Wallis, Salisbury, Wiltshire. **Photographic acknowledgements:** Alamy Antiques & Collectables 76; David Kilpatrick 115; Danita Delimont 191 al; Decorative Arts 206; Elizabeth Whiting & Associates 120, 128, 138, 198; Hemis 175; Jeremy Evans 191 br; Joe Tree 191 ar; John Glover 190; Mark Fiennes/Arcaid 134; Mike Booth 167; National Trust Photolibrary 136 a; Robert Harding Picture Library Ltd 209; Tony French 191 bl; Travelshots.com 62; TravelStockCollection/Homer Sykes 194; V&A Images 208; Arcaid Alan Weintraub/© DACS 2010 170 a; Michael Banks 6 b; 182 a; Bridgeman Art Library Brooklyn Museum of Art, New York, USA/Gift of Raymond Worgelt 140; Ickworth, Suffolk, UK/National Trust Photographic Library 147; Tim Clinch 57; Corbis Abode/Beateworks 55; Adrian Wilson/Beateworks 38; Edifice/© FLC/ADAGP, Paris and DACS, London 2010 171; Elizabeth Whiting & Associates 61, 170 b; Historical Picture Archive 161 a; James Mitchell 44; Kate Kunz 200; Ludovic Maisant 162 b; Massimo Listri 151; Mimmo Jodice 162 a; Roy Morsch 116; Steve Hawkins/Elizabeth Whiting & Associates 163; Steven Vidler/Eurasia Press 186; Trevor Mein/Arcaid 81; Ercol Butterfly chair 77 c; Roger Gain178; Geffrye Museum, London 166 b; Getty Images Peter Harholdt 144; Oli Scarff 197; Trine Thorsen/Red Cover 87a; Mark Hill 188; Peter Marshall 52; 58; 59; 142 a; James Merrell 31; 142 b; 146 b; 154 a & b; 158 b; Neil Mersh 12; 14; 23; 43; 54; 178 b; National Trust Photo Library Andreas von Einsiedel 150 a; Dennis Gilbert 166 a; Nadia Mackenzie 155, 159; Red Cover Guglielmo Galvin 91; Ken Hayden, architect Rene Gonzales 35, designer Juan Montoya 60; Lucinda Symons 28; Simon Scarboro 80; Didi von Schaewen 26; 39; 42; 46; 47; 50; 51; 75; 143; 146 top; 179; 183. All other images are copyright Octopus Publishing Group Ltd

First published in Great Britain in 2010 by Mitchell Beazley,
an imprint of Octopus Publishing Group Ltd, Endeavour House,
189 Shaftesbury Avenue, London, WC2H 8JG.
www.hachette.co.uk

ISBN 978 1 84533 556 4

A CIP record for this book is available from the British Library

Editorial Director Tracey Smith **Publishing Manager** Julie Brooke
General Editorial Consultants Corrine Ochiltree, Lesley Malkin, Mark Hill
Consultant Editor (Antiques) Anna Southgate
Consultant Editor (Interiors) Caroline Wheater
Copy Editor Alison Wormleighton
Proofreader Clare Hacking **Indexer** Isobel McLean

Art Director and Jacket Design Pene Parker
Design Yasia Williams-Leedham, David Rowley
Photography Hugh Gilbert **Picture Research** Giulia Hetherington
Production Peter Hunt, Carolin Stransky

Warning: Please take every care when handling chemicals and undertaking the renovation techniques detailed in 'Reviving Antiques'. Follow appropriate safety procedures and keep all dangerous substances in a safe place, away from children and animals and where they cannot be used in error. Wear protective clothing and goggles whenever relevant. The Publishers cannot be held responsible for any damage to persons or property that may occur from using this book and the opinions expressed within it are not necessarily those of the Publisher.

CONTENTS

INTRODUCTION

We see it as a rebirth. Not only of an interest in and love for antiques, but also of people truly expressing themselves in their homes. More and more of us seem to have become a bit bored and fed up with bland furniture and interiors promoted by retail park or high street chain stores who push their catalogues through our doors. There's more to life than a flat-pack chipboard bookcase. However useful it might be, everyone we know owns one, or something like it. It doesn't say much about us and who we are, does it?

On the other hand, you might own something inherited. Or something picked up in a junk shop or flea market as close as Preston, as romantic as Paris, or as far-flung as Phuket. It still holds a story about you. What attracted you to that particular piece? What did it say to you when you first saw it? Did it call out to you?

Not only that, but there's the story behind a piece, be it the wear and tear of decades or centuries of love and attention, or the initials of a mysterious previous owner. How many and what kind of celebrations has a Georgian decanter seen before it graces your dinner table? Where was it when Queen Victoria was crowned? Who owned it when World War II broke out? Who poured wine from it, and what did the wine taste like? Antique and vintage pieces give you a wealth of stories that new items simply can't.

Many think that the mix between and new and old is not a happy marriage, but the look is becoming ever more popular. And it's not difficult to achieve. The key thread is our personal relationship with an object. It might be an incredibly comfortable inherited armchair, a particularly warming shade of red, or a cup and saucer that reminds us of a much-loved relative. Think of yourself – your story – and be bold.

Our job is to take antiques off their pedestal. They're living, breathing things that can become much-loved and well-used parts of the family. They needn't be restricted to display on the top shelf of a cupboard and only brought out on "high days and holidays" for people to gasp at in admiration. We've reflected this in the six rooms we created for different families across the country while making the television series that accompanies this book – we hope they will act as an inspiration for you to do the same. (Photographs of these rooms have been spread throughout the book, and can be identified using the list on page 224.)

Craftsmanship is another factor that makes old better than new. How many times have we cursed at a flat-pack piece as we try to put it up, only to curse at it again when it collapses? This doesn't happen with solid wood antique or vintage furniture, which has withstood decades, or even centuries, of use. If something has lasted for this long, then it can certainly stand up to the rigours of modern life. The old cliché that "they don't build them like they used to" is most certainly true.

But value doesn't just apply to craftsmanship and emotional value. We believe that antiques are better for your pocket. The downturn of interest in traditional wooden furniture over the past ten years has meant that demand has plummeted, together with prices. There truly has never been a better time to buy. A solid mahogany chest of drawers from the 19th century can be had for as little as £300-£500. A single Victorian balloon-back chair can become part of a characterful "harlequin" set for under £30, and eye-catching Art Deco ceramics can be picked up for a song. Compare that to their equivalents on the high street and they look great value – as well as being typically more stylish.

Unlike most new pieces, antiques also have a resale value. If you can ever bear to part with a piece, if you chose wisely, you're more than likely to be able to get your money back. You may even make a profit. You can't say that about an MDF bookcase or wardrobe.

Antiques are green. The vast majority are made from solid wood. The warmth of colour and variety of the grain, from a 1960s Scandinavian teak dining table to a Georgian "flame" mahogany sideboard, or the exquisite elegance of fruitwood inlay cannot be matched by MDF, chipboard or mass-produced yellow pine. This beautiful wood has not been taken from felled foreign forests, shipped to a factory for assembly and then shipped across the world for sale. Most modern furniture has a carbon footprint the size of a sub-continent, and we have to question the ethics of how most of this was produced, and who by. And talking of being eco-friendly, the buzz-word of the moment for us is "repurposing". The ultimate in glamorous recycling, there's something magical about taking an unloved and often unwanted item and transforming it into a one off "haute couture" piece, tailor-made not only for the space in which it sits, but also for the person who made it. With perhaps only a lick of paint and a bit of TLC, it's a truly satisfying thing to do especially when times are tough and money's tight. If you get good at it, it may even be a way of making a bit of extra cash.

The recession has been hard on us as a nation, but out of hardship often comes great ingenuity and a flourish of creative imagination. Because it's harder to sell our houses now, we can ditch the "blank canvas" magnolia filled houses we've all been living in. We've been given permission to express our personalities in how we fill and live in our homes – an uplifting and liberating experience. And the best and often cheapest way of doing this, to fight the homogeny, is to buy old rather than new.

We hope that our TV series and the book you hold in your hands will encourage and empower you to buy and live with antiques. Although it appears intimidating, armed with a bit of practical knowledge, the world of antiques can be enjoyed by everyone, regardless of personal taste or budget. There's so much to discover. So, grab this book and a wad of cash and get out there. Good luck!

Kathryn Rayward & Mark Hill

LIVING WITH ANTIQUES

LIVING ROOMS

Previous page: *A Victorian-style living room with a dining area, in a turn-of-the-century terraced house. Note the Art Nouveau stained glass in the windows, which are original.*

Opposite: *Neo-Classical and Art Deco sculpture form a centrepiece enhanced by a glass chandelier and porter's chair which is framed by two full-length windows. The window frames are surmounted by Venetian mirrored panels, which echo the chandelier and add an opulent feel.*

Whether your home is large or small, urban or rural, antiques and vintage pieces add a feeling of quality and individuality to your interior style. Your living room is the ideal place to begin experimenting with a more eclectic or period look. To start with, the living room is usually one of the biggest rooms in the house, there will probably be large windows to allow in plenty of light to illuminate your favourite buys and plenty of wall space to accommodate them.

The beautiful high-ceilinged room pictured opposite is a space of calm and restraint. Floor-to-ceiling windows allow light to flood in to create a naturally uplifting atmosphere. Decoratively, the style of the room is understated, with pale ivory walls and glimmering silk curtains that enhance the architecture and reflect light back into the darker areas of the room. A touch of colour in the blue patterned rug stops the look from becoming too drab, and an element of glamour is added by the Venetian-style mirrored glass pelmets and chandelier. The room has been furnished along early 19th-century Neo-classical lines, with painted Swedish upholstered chairs in muted grey fabric complementing a highly polished oval table with similar sabre-shaped legs. A gorgeous, dark brown leather hooded chair, designed to keep out draughts, is the surprise in the mix; its contrasting style makes it a focal point, with the eye drawn in by the symmetrical layout of the other furniture around it. The choice of antique ornaments – odd numbers of things are more pleasing to the eye than even numbers – proves that less really can be more.

Above: Echoing the curves of the coffee table, designed by Isamu Noguchi in 1944, the large pebbles in the living room above contrast with the angular lines of the lacquered furniture behind. The wood panelled wall adds a feeling of warmth to the room.

Opposite: Georgian demi-lune tables, a French rococo–style low stool, upholstered sofas, and a faux-bamboo chair are combined in this Victorian-inspired living room. The deep cushions and welcoming fire help to create a cosy atmosphere.

A living room is naturally warm and inviting: the place you want to read a book, take a snooze, or entertain friends. The two interior schemes pictured here have very different styles but are both from the "more is more" corner, creating a rich, cosy feel. Interestingly, the colourful painted walls act as the unifying element in both schemes – one distinctly Victorian, the other a tribute to Mid-century Modern style.

In the classic scheme shown opposite the mustard walls offset a riot of patterns, fabric, furniture, and objects, from flowery chintz sofas to Regency-style drapes to antique ceramics on the mantelpiece. These possessions could clash, but they sit harmoniously because the plain wall colour acts as a blank canvas.

The elegant marble fireplace is the focal point of the room, enhanced by a gilded oval mirror – a shape that softens the masculine lines of the carved stone. There is pleasing symmetry here too, with a pair of demi-lune tables by the fireplace, and a sofa either side.

In the Mid-century Modern room above, the yellow wall creates a quirky touch to enliven a small space. Contemporary and 1950s-1960s Scandinavian ceramics and an abstract animal-print rug provide eccentric partners to an outdoorsy, white metal chair. An interesting feature in this room is the fact that there is no fireplace, instead a low-level shelf unit draws the eye and in turn becomes a focal point of interest.

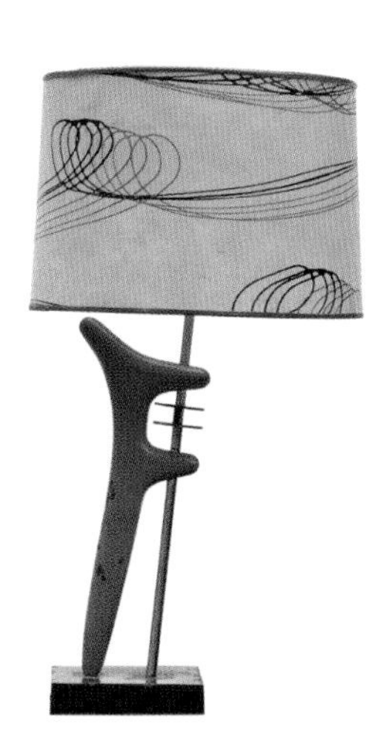

LIVING ROOM ANTIQUES

Above right: *1930s Art Deco leather club armchairs are highly sought-after, particularly in such good condition (see p71). Arched backs and deep arms are desirable features to look out for.*

Above: *The biomorphic and asymmetric form of this 1950s American lacquered metal lampbase is typical of the period. The original paper shade is rare.*

Right: *Designed by George Nelson in 1955, the form of the 'Coconut' chair echoes slices of a coconut shell. It is minimal in both its form and use of limited materials.*

Vintage furniture offers robust, well-made pieces that are ideal for these much-used rooms. Comfort is key and can be found readily in Victorian sofas, with their deep-buttoned, coil-sprung upholstery, and in body-sculpted 1950s lounge chairs. Storage pieces made using traditional cabinet-making techniques are extremely durable and can be found in good condition. The Coconut chair shown below is wide enough to provide the sitter with room to curl up or to perch with their legs crossed, providing casual and comfortable seating. The rich colours of such woods as walnut, oak, teak, and mahogany bring a welcome warmth to the living room. Wood can be complemented by vintage leather club armchairs, leather being one of the few upholstery choices that improve with age.

BETTER TO BUY OLD THAN NEW

The epitome of opulence and luxury living, the Victorian chaise longue is a perfect focal piece for the modern living room. With its solid mahogany frame, this beautifully constructed piece is arguably better value than one from the high street, and can be re-upholstered time and again to suit your changing tastes – a huge advantage over many modern pieces. A seminal design for its time, and originally made in pairs, the chaise longue is unlikely to go out of fashion and is likely to hold its value.

A Victorian mahogany and gold velvet button-upholstered chaise longue, made c1870, and worth £500-700, is ripe for renovation. Examples can sometimes be found for less.

Left: *Teak, with its warm colour and beautiful grain, was favoured by Mid-century Modern Scandinavian designers. The undecorated surfaces of this 1950s unit by Hans Wegner show the wood off at its best.*

Below: *Tiled tables were popular from the 1950s-60s. The curving, asymmetric form and tapered legs are typical of the period.*

FOCUS ON: POSTMODERN DESIGN

Starting as a radical reaction to what designers considered the banality of Modernism, Postmodern design became the defining look of the last quarter of the 20th century, permeating all aspects of architecture and the decorative arts. With roots in 1970s Italy, and the establishment of a number of "anti-design" groups – such as Alessandro Mendini's Studio Alchimia and its more commercially successful splinter group, Memphis, under the direction of Ettore Sottsass – this new style demonstrated an ironic, often irreverent approach to design. While Mendini was intent on producing one-off pieces, almost as works of art, Sottsass and his like-minded contemporaries relished the idea of having their creations reproduced, albeit in limited numbers.

Brash and bright and colourful, their furniture, glassware, ceramics, and lighting designs defied the tenets of "form follows function" and "good design" that had dominated the post-war years. Borrowing liberally from the past, they reappropriated Classical architectural and historical forms and motifs, using them alongside unlikely juxtapositions of materials (fine timbers combined with plastic laminates, for example). Forms were deliberately awkward, asymmetrical, and uneasy on the eye. In complete opposition to Modernist design, the emphasis shifted from the function of a piece to its eyebrow-raising appearance.

Alongside Ettore Sottsass, the Memphis designers included Michele de Lucchi, Michael Graves, Andrea Branzi, and George Sowden. Their designs met with international acclaim and inspired a whole generation of designers. It was not long before Postmodern design was adopted as a style during the 1980s and early 1990s by companies as diverse as Alessi, Swatch, Knoll and Swid Powell.

Although this style may currently be out of fashion, Postmodernism had too great an impact to be overlooked for much longer. In fact, a number of design gurus have already started to seek out examples. If you are thinking of doing the same, look for pieces that exemplify the main characteristics of the style – bold use of colour, unlikely juxtaposition of shapes, patterned plastic laminates. The very best items were made in small numbers and were expensive for their time, so buy now before prices rise further. Smaller pieces, such as items from Rosenthal's "Flash" ceramics designed by Dorothy Hafner in 1982 can currently be found for under £200.

Above: Designed by Ettore Sottsass in the mid–1960s, and produced by Flavia in Italy, this is part of a range of 'totem' sculptures. A colourful Postmodern icon, they contrasted Western Pop Art and materialism against Indian spirituality.

Right: Some Postmodern forms have animal-like forms, such as this 'Tahiti' lamp designed by Ettore Sottsass for Memphis in 1981.

GET THE LOOK FOR LESS

In the field of Postmodern ceramics, the New York firm Swid Powell was quick to seize the day. Founded in 1983, the company commissioned leading international architects, such as Robert Venturi, Ettore Sottsass and Zaha Hadid, to contribute designs for its high-quality tablewares. This example, from Venturi's "Grandmother" series, satirizes the dated florals that many of us associate with "Granny". Original pieces carry a facsimile of the designer's signature on the back, along with the company name and series title. Prices typically range from £40-120, which is inexpensive compared to furniture and many other pieces. The market is new and examples are often passed over or ignored, meaning bargains can be found. If interest continues to grow, these may prove to be a wise investment.

An American Swid Powell transfer-printed 'Grandmother' pattern ceramic plate, designed by Robert Venturi in 1984.

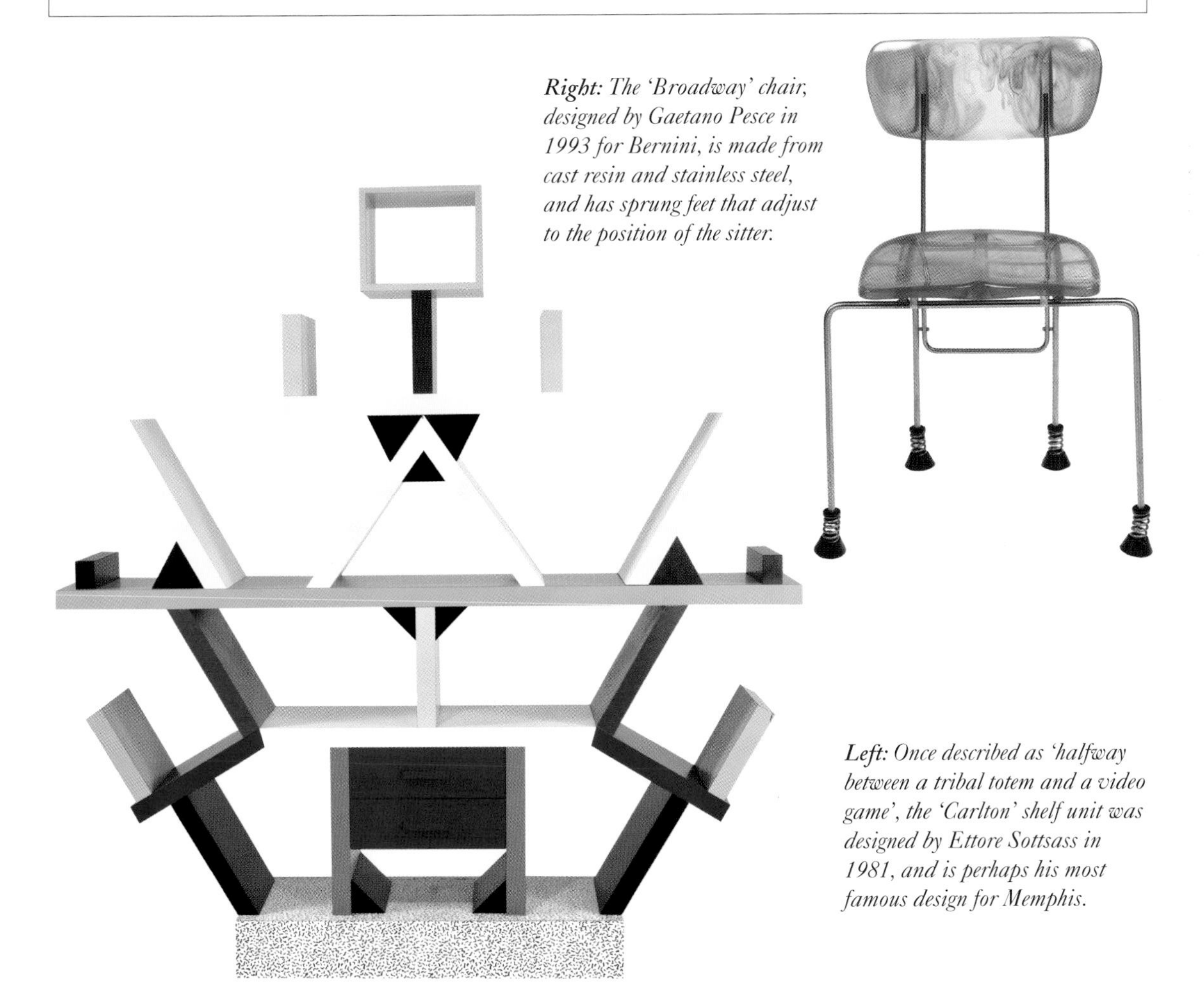

***Right:** The 'Broadway' chair, designed by Gaetano Pesce in 1993 for Bernini, is made from cast resin and stainless steel, and has sprung feet that adjust to the position of the sitter.*

***Left:** Once described as 'halfway between a tribal totem and a video game', the 'Carlton' shelf unit was designed by Ettore Sottsass in 1981, and is perhaps his most famous design for Memphis.*

DINING ROOMS

Opposite: You needn't be slavish to a look. This 21st century take on a Georgian dining room includes an Edwardian Georgian-style table, six mid-19th century balloon-back chairs, and Regency wine decanters. The paint colour and wallpaper are inspired by Georgian examples.

Dining has become less formal over the years and yet nothing beats sitting around a table to talk and exchange news and views. The ritual of dining gives design lovers plenty of scope to try out ideas and change their style from meal to meal, whether it's teaming a classic 1930s dinner service with antique wineglasses, or taking the 1960s route with a Le Creuset casserole and much-loved Denby stoneware, or making up individual place settings of non-matching china. This is your opportunity to show off vintage coffee cups, and simply engraved Victorian glasses for liqueurs. For magpie collectors dining is an opportunity to make the tableware a talking point.

Buying antique or vintage furnishings increases the note of individuality that can be achieved in a room scheme – far more so than if a table and chairs are a matching suite. The chairs around the table shown in the room opposite are actually not from the same original set but they do match in terms of shape. In this way a unified atmosphere has been maintained, without the extra expense of trying to buy a set of chairs from the same original set – which is a particularly expensive exercise if you want to own more than four of them. There is another advantage to buying vintage or antique over new. The wood used is likely to be of a much better quality than that used for mass-made contemporary pieces and may even be of a type that is unaffordable now, such as rosewood, teak, or mahogany. Standards of craftsmanship will probably also be much higher than those of contemporary pieces of comparable price.

As a space for entertaining guests, the dining room is a place where you can afford to be a little more flamboyant and stamp your style.

***Above:** The gentle Neo-rococo curves of the iron 'Spine' chair designed by Jean Dubrueil in 1988 contrast against the hard lines of Jean Prouvé's chairs of 1942, and the 'Mexique' shelf unit designed by Prouvé and Charlotte Perriand in 1953.*

As a space for entertaining guests, the dining room is somewhere you can afford to be a little more flamboyant and stamp your style. Dining rooms are ideal for mixing and matching furnishing materials and finishes, as proved by this striking pairing of a contemporary granite-topped table (above) with Modernist plywood and metal chairs. Though of completely different origin and date, the table and chairs fit well together because they are similar in design – very linear and with strong-looking sabre legs. Sometimes it pays to be brave when choosing things, and it is worth pushing your own boundaries of taste to create a striking scheme.

Big and bold is the style of this room, from the dining suite to the large contemporary canvas mounted above it, the eccentric metal chair, and the

practical bookcase cum shelving unit. An interior scheme such as this begs for some stylish contemporary light fixtures that are designed as wall sculptures. Interestingly, the room has a powerful visual impact despite containing relatively few things. In this case less is more because the furnishings are all eye-catching in their own right.

When not in use, a dining table is a great place for displaying other treasures such as the sculptural metal candlesticks designed by Luigi Colani, which also reflect pleasingly in the shiny stone table-top. Large pottery bowls, candelabras, and vases are other finishing touches to consider. Place them slightly off-centre to catch the eye – instinctively we love shapes that mimic the slightly more random and less regular or symmetrical character of some of the forms found in the world of nature.

DINING ROOM ANTIQUES

__Above right:__ A heavier feel and turned legs are typical features of early 19th century sideboards, such as this Regency mahogany bowfront example.

__Above:__ The serpentine fronts and lids inlaid with boxwood urns on this pair of late 18th century mahogany knife boxes are typical of Georgian elegance. They open to reveal fitted storage for cutlery.

__Right:__ The futuristic form and use of steel and smoked glass on this 1970s table update the traditional pedestal table. It would also suit an Art Deco interior perfectly.

Georgian and Regency dining furniture captures perfectly the element of elegance and formality that many of us seek in the dining room. Rich woods such as mahogany and rosewood reflect the warm, soft tones that suit entertaining by candlelight. A good number of tables from the 18th and early 19th centuries have leaves that can be removed or slotted in depending on the number of guests, without spoiling the integrity of the piece. Elegant sideboards offer essential storage for your prized Victorian dinner service, but are also the perfect place to show off the family silver or a collection of sparkling, cut-glass decanters. Sets of mahogany dining chairs are easily found to complement the look.

BETTER TO BUY OLD THAN NEW

At around £150 a piece, this pair of Chippendale Revival mahogany dining chairs represent incredible value for money compared with the majority of modern-day equivalents – and are also more likely to hold their value. Well-constructed with beautifully carved splats, the chairs are typical of Chippendale's early 18th-century Gothic designs. Look out for a set with a pair of carvers to place at the ends of the table. Generously proportioned, the drop-in seats also allow you to change the upholstery easily and cheaply, making the chairs a great long-term purchase.

Right: Designed by Frenchman Maurice Pre, this 1950s set of dining chairs have clean, Modern forms and are made from waxed oak. Both features are typical of Pre's work, and a set of six is highly desirable.

FOCUS ON: USING COLOUR

Colour is the interior decorator's most versatile tool for creating atmosphere, mood, and period style. For a calm, restful scheme, opt for lighter, pastel colours – leaf green, primrose yellow, pale pink, and powder blue. If it's passion and energy that appeal, choose rich tones such as deep purple, scarlet, tangerine, and fuchsia.

The paint colour palettes available today are impressive, ranging from a variety of historical collections through Art Deco metallics to contemporary pastels. Additionally, paint effects such as ragging, sponging, dragging, and marbling can mimic the look of old walls, limewashing, or antique surfaces.

You can achieve a sense of drama in various ways. Deep, rich colours are the classic route. Use them singly on walls for maximum impact, or be experimental and create a patchwork of colours that sit well together – test on large sheets of paper first. Remember that dark colours absorb light, so it's as well to choose a room with plenty of windows to carry out this look. If you like a splash of colour but not too much, use a darker accent colour here and there, on a feature wall perhaps, or a painted shelf or a chair.

Below: Majestic deep blue wallpaper with a repeated pattern or gold fleur-de-lys provides a backdrop for a gilded pediment and throne-like open armchair.

More restrained schemes can look just as striking, if a little more elegant. A palette of soft browns, bronzes, and greys will complement antique furniture and objects. Use darker shades at the bottom of walls to help anchor the room and lighter shades toward the ceiling to add a feeling of spaciousness and light. Pale colours reflect light and so are better if you want to create an airy, fresh feel. If you have low ceilings paint them in a pale hue or brilliant white to create the illusion of greater height. Your choice of finish is very important too. For a soft and lived-in feel, always opt for a matt chalky emulsion.

Wallpaper is a fabulous way of introducing colour to a room, even if it's restricted to appearing on just one wall. Large patterns look better in big rooms and carry more impact, whereas smaller floral or geometrical patterns suit corridors, entrance halls, or minor rooms although breaking the rules every so often can make invigorating and striking schemes. Many new wallpapers were inspired by old designs but have been updated, meaning you can achieve the style you want without a room looking fusty. Metallics are currently very fashionable and can add light and depth to a room by bouncing light off their surface.

ENLARGED IMAGES

Customizing interiors to achieve a more individual look is becoming easier with the evolution of digital photography. Not only can we buy large photographic canvases from high street stores at great prices, but bespoke companies have gone one step further, printing images of your choice onto plain wallpaper rolls or giant canvases. The result is big, bold, and brilliant, taking the idea of wall art onto another plane. Landscape scenes, trees, flowers, butterflies – all can be the backdrops to everyday life. In the room shown here, a print of the London skyline has been enlarged to great effect, producing an almost abstract pattern that is as intriguing as it is beautiful.

Jack Baymoore
Bandits

KITCHENS

__Opposite:__ 1950s wire furniture and accessories enhance a light, bright kitchen. Add in a collage of photographs of Elvis Presley and the scene is set for a rocking and rolling breakfast.

Not every house is blessed with a dining room, and for smaller homes or homes with an open-plan layout, the kitchen-diner is an essential space. We spend so much time in the kitchen that it often becomes one of the favourite rooms in the house and deserves to be treated as such. This is the place to have a bit of fun decorating and furnishing – after all, it greets us first thing in the morning and bids us goodnight after a hard day's work.

The decorative style of the 1950s gives a kitchen-diner bags of character, as the interior opposite shows. Jaunty period colours such as butter yellow, mint green, and pastel blue teamed with clean, hygienic white give a fresh look that is a pleasure to be in, whether you are sipping a cup of coffee or getting creative with recipes.

A small space benefits from built-in cupboards, which were popular in the 1930s as well as the 1950s. The kind of shelving in such cupboards has room for both hiding things away and putting other things on show – favourite mugs and jugs, a collection of vintage storage jars, or some classic cookbooks. Popular as a material in the period, as well as being easy to clean, Formica is used here for a breakfast bar, continuing the look. Checked floor tiles add wow factor from the bottom up. Gorgeous vintage linen tea towels not only look good but are often a better quality weave than anything made today. If, after hanging these up, you have any more space, put up a vintage wall clock or a wall decoration to add a focal point to an otherwise blank space. It is such details that add real authentic character to a room and searching them out in boot fairs, secondhand shops and even your relatives' cupboards will be enjoyable and well worth the effort.

Above: *An antique French painted cupboard, a 'harlequin' set of chairs, floral ceramics, and even a church pew, add an interesting, eclectic edge to this country-style dining area.*

Furnishing a big kitchen with antiques can easily create a period look that harks back to Victorian or Edwardian days without being a pastiche. The kitchen pictured above right has a classic feel but is contemporary in its decorating scheme of slate and cream.

First there are some obvious must-haves, such as a traditional-style stoneware sink and a range cooker. Classic butler's sinks are to be found in most salvage yards but watch out for chips and cracks as they can be expensive to put right. Old ranges can also be sourced but tend to be bought for their decorative appeal. Installing a new but traditional-style range is the most practical answer for modern-day home-owners.

Above: An Aga and a butler's sink are traditional kitchen items. Bring them up to date with glazed fitted cabinets and collectable 20th century studio pottery bowls.

All kitchens need somewhere to put precious collections, and glazed wall cupboards are perfect for this . This is the place to put kitchenalia such as jelly moulds, pressed glass, cranberry glass, and teapots dating from the Victorian era up to the 1930s. Indulge your personal passions by searching for treasures in second-hand shops and boot fairs. Old wooden spoons and utensils also look the part, along with vintage coffee grinders, weighing scales, and copper kettles. As always, its the small details that can make all the difference, so it's worth spending time ferreting out old hardware, handles, and knobs from secondhand shops, boot fairs and architectural salvage suppliers so that you get the right period look.

KITCHEN ANTIQUES

Hard-working functional rooms, kitchens are as well suited to robust country-style furniture as they are to streamlined Modernist forms. Space is usually at a premium, so a large free-standing oak or pine dresser can be a useful investment (and can cost significantly less than the equivalent built-in cabinets). Rustic pieces, such as scrubbed pine tables, offer ideal work surfaces. Not only are they more attractive than modern-day plastic and Formica alternatives, but they also double up as convivial eating places for less formal meals. Small-scale Mid-century Modern furniture and 1960s stainless steel kitchen wares, with their sleek and functional designs, complement the look and function of the room beautifully.

VINTAGE CLASSICS

Arne Jacobsen's 1955 "Mosquito" chair is one of several designs that fall under the iconic 1950s "Series 7" umbrella. The beauty of these chairs and their suitability for kitchen use are manifold. Primarily they are small and take up very little room, with the fact that they stack making them even more economical on space. The minimal design of the chair means that it will work with any number of different styles of kitchen. The laminated wood bends for comfort, and is also extremely durable and easy to clean. Avoid modern imitations, which are generally of poorer quality.

Far left: *Dressers have fallen out of fashion with many, but are decorative as well as functional. The carved decoration on this late Georgian oak dresser is appealing. Try displaying blue and white ceramics on the shelves for an instant country kitchen feel.*

Left: *Country chairs are typically made from indigenous woods, such as elm and beech, as with this Victorian stickback example.*

Bottom left: *This minimal, stainless steel coffee pot is part of Stelton's 'Cylinda' line of Modernist kitchenware, designed by architect Arne Jacobsen around 1967.*

Right: *Floral chintz tablewares, such as this printed cake stand, were popular from the 1930s to the 1950s. The Art Deco style plastic handle, chrome fittings and gold pattern dates this example to the 1930s-40s.*

FOCUS ON: DISPLAYING GLASS

Of all the crafts, glass is one of the most popular areas of collecting: it is plentiful, it can be found in an extraordinary range of colours and forms, it reflects light and sparkles to delight the eye and pieces can be secured inexpensively from so many different periods, with many beautiful studio pieces also being produced today by modern glassmakers. In essence a domestic item, glass has a natural affinity with the home and can be used to with great effect to dress any room.

However limited your space, there is always room for some glass, from luxurious perfume bottles to giant bowls and vases. Glass looks at its best set on glass. A glass-topped coffee table can become the heart of a room when arranged with a beautiful collection because the assortment and reflections will draw the eye.

One of the most effective ways of grouping glass is to do it vertically on a shelf unit, on floating shelves, or on a shelved room divider (see opposite). Arranging by colour creates a common theme and ties pieces together even if they are of different sizes and from different eras. Arranging by shapes such as tall, round or square looks good and will give cohesion to different coloured items. If history is your passion, arranging by style and era, such as Georgian wine glasses or 1960s Murano glass, will give the collection a narrative element.

Left: *The wall colour unites the varied selection of glass which comprises 1950s-60s Italian display goblets and a Victorian style pressed glass dessert bowl. Modern, clean lines add variety to a traditional interior.*

BREAKING THE RULES

The true glory of glass can only be seen when its colour and pattern are illuminated. If you have a south-facing window with a deep sill, arrange some glass pieces on it and let the sunshine do the work for you. In a room with less natural light, direct one or two spotlights onto a single piece or small group of glass. Another option, as seen here, is to design a custom cabinet or shelf system for displaying studio glass, with integral spotlights that illuminate a piece from above and below, making it glow.

A white cabinet with customised lighting allows the craftsmanship of the glassmakers who made these vases to shine, and the vibrant colours to come alive.

BEDROOMS

***Opposite:** Strong colour contrasts with delicate white in bold planes, providing the perfect foil for showing off Rococo curves. The early 20th century French chaise longue invites you to recline and relax.*

A private retreat, an intimate space, and a buffer zone of creature comforts, the bedroom is a blank canvas where more dramatic interior tastes can be indulged. Planning an interior scheme for a bedroom is an opportunity to please no one but yourself.

The bed, being bigger than anything else in the room, will be the first piece of furniture to consider. Antique and reproduction beds come in all shapes and sizes, from Victorian brass frames and solid Arts and Crafts examples to sleigh beds and four-posters – anything goes. Or you could "antique" a modern headboard by covering it with some vintage fabric, or layer vintage quilts and rugs for a period look. Heavy Welsh blankets, toile de Jouy bedspreads, antique patchwork, or vintage linen will do the trick.

As the room pictured shows, you can be as eclectic as you like with the choice of accessories, including Continental candlesticks from a church, a Louis XVI style bedside table, a 20th century French traditional chandelier, and so on. The more diverse the items on show, the richer the effect.

Although dressing tables were out of fashion for several decades, they are bang on trend again, and for many women they are both a must-have and a treat – somewhere to sit and prepare for the day (or the evening!) ahead, and to store lotions and potions. The 1930s and the 1950s were fruitful decades for dressing tables, which very often came with integral mirrors, and you may find bargains lurking at auction houses and antiques fairs. To add to the relaxing feel of your bedroom, you could even invest in a small Edwardian salon sofa, and a small oak bookcase for storing bedside novels.

Above: *A contemporary wrought iron bed contrasts with Swedish Gustavian-style bedside cabinet and armchair and a classic French armoire. Neutral walls and bedlinens add to the airy feel of the room.*

Patterned fabric and dramatic colour can be used to great effect as the flamboyantly decorated bedrooms pictured here demonstrate. The key to creating impact is to restrict the colour palette to one or two main colours of a similar tone. Pillows, throws, and curtains all contribute to a Bohemian air of comfort and indulgence. In the opulent bedroom opposite, the elegant interior draws strongly on 18th-century style, with every surface and ornament contributing to the look. At night an exotic toile de Jouy canopy over the bed makes the occupant feel snug and cosseted, and then during daylight hours it transforms into a sumptuous daybed, scattered with large pillows.

The European Grand Tour look is continued in the small statues, classical plaster friezes over the door and near the bed, and collection of 19th-century portraits, portrait miniatures, and carved medals mounted on the walls. Light is provided by an equally dramatic source, a large chandelier, with candle sconces casting romantic shadows on the walls.

To complete the look the owner has used dark wood furniture, such as a table and cupboard in mahogany or dark-stained oak, to display porcelain and plaster busts. A smattering of painted furniture stops the sheer richness of the room from becoming too overpowering and indicates a lightness of touch.

Above: *Snug bed or opulent day bed – this luxurious bedroom shows how antiques can be used to create a sumptuous interior.*

BEDROOM ANTIQUES

Striking Empire, Regency, and Biedermeier period beds offer a welcome return to luxury that is all too often lost in modern-day designs. The beds stand just as proud in minimalist surroundings as in more exuberant schemes, and can be found at competitive prices. More feminine pieces – elegant Art Nouveau dressing tables and Mid-century Modern vanity mirrors – are economical on space, often an important consideration. Traditionally handcrafted Arts and Crafts coffers, bedside cabinets, and rocking chairs are devoid of superficial decoration. The rich, warm colours of their solid oak surfaces offer the perfect backdrop for beautifully coloured and textured vintage fabrics or simple unbleached linen.

Above left: *The carving on this American oak armchair, c1900, is for the 'The Odd Fellows' friendly society. Links such as this add interest, and can add value, to a piece.*

Above right: *British furniture company Harris Lebus was well-known for bedroom furniture, especially in the Arts and Crafts style, such as this dressing table, c1905.*

Right: *The Neoclassical opulence of Napoleon's France is recalled in this mahogany bed.*

BETTER TO BUY OLD THAN NEW

Antique and vintage mirrors can be found for a fraction of the cost of a new, high-street equivalent. Size matters, and the larger and bolder the statement, the better. Reflective surfaces from before the mid-19th century were made using an amalgam of tin and mercury, which adds warmth and depth to the reflection. After the 1920s, aluminium was used. If gilding is damaged, this can be touched up with gilt cream, but do not be afraid to paint a frame, as with the mirror on the right, if it is in poor condition.

Left: *Unblemished surfaces and simple forms allow the grain of the birch to sing on these 1950s Continental wardrobes.*

Below: *This German enamelled wood and steel dressing table and stool evoke the space age designs of Verner Panton, and the vibrant colours of the 1960s.*

MAKING THE BED

The bed is such a large piece of furniture that it seems a shame not to make the most of it. A headboard can be transformed overnight into something more interesting and stylish by covering it in a piece of vintage fabric such as toile de Jouy or patterned linen, or painting it a pretty colour and stencilling with classic motifs. The best beds look plump and generously made up, so the choice of bed linen is crucial. Use Oxford pillows and large pillows at the head of the bed to create a sumptuous look, and raise the height of the mattress with a comfy topper. Finish the look with a toning quilt or bedspread laid over sheets and blankets that hide the bed frame as they drop toward the floor. You can't beat a bolster to add to the general luxuriance of a lavish bed

Comfort underfoot is an essential part of bedroom decor, so be liberal with rugs. Building on the textile theme, fabric wall hangings bring warmth and interest to plain walls – blend contemporary woven textiles with small silk rugs, vintage scarves, and swatches of antique fabric that can be easily framed.

Consider the lighting carefully. A chandelier, whether old or new, is the ultimate in glamour. For soft light in the evenings, invest in some lamps. A floor lamp is useful for working at a desk or reading in an armchair. The style of lamps set by the bed can complement the bed linen and furniture, but make sure they are tall enough to allow for reading in bed. Introduce a mirror to reflect light around the room.

Opposite: *Piles of pillows, layers of blankets and a tented fabric ceiling soften the geometric lines of this room. The circles of the PH5 pendant lamp, designed by Poul Henningsen in 1958, and the Classical cast at the head of the bed echo the porthole window.*

An opulent gilded starburst headboard and faux fur throw contrast with bare wooden floorboards.

DRAMATIC EFFECTS

Secret and snug, the bedroom is the perfect place to go a bit over the top and create an interior scheme with wow factor. Keep wall art to a minimum and invest in just one stunning thing to go above the bed. It could, for example, be a Classical plaster frieze, a fan of ostrich feathers, or a glamorous Hollywood starlet headboard in a starburst shape upholstered in tactile velvet. If the piece is big enough and bold enough, it's the only statement you'll need.

BATHROOMS

***Opposite:** Simply, yet cleverly, painting the outside of the roll top bath the same colour as the walls allows the eye to rest naturally on the 'wow factor' in the room – the beautifully upholstered Victorian chaise longue.*

Counterbalance the fast pace of living with an enticing bathroom to unwind in. Though bathroom "furniture" – baths, basins, toilets – has a basic shape and purpose, it comes in a range of period styles. This allows decorating ideas to flow in whichever direction you want, from classic Victorian and Edwardian to glamorous Art Deco or stern, masculine modernist. Antique baths and sinks are widely available at salvage yards; once the right shape has been sourced, yards will usually finish an item to the customer's specification.
In the spacious and luxurious bathroom pictured opposite, the shape of the feet of the Vintage roll-top bath echo the feel of the Victorian chaise longue, whilst the use of chrome and the grey and white walls add an Art Deco contemporary feel that's bang up to date.
The advantage of using a larger room as a bathroom is that you can fit more furniture and features into it, creating a stronger period ambience. Here a small fireplace will provide extra warmth during an evening soak, and a vintage rug adds to the overall feeling of relaxation. There's room, too, for a couple of armchairs with slipcovers and a 20th-century piecrust table that has been painted white and transformed into a towel holder. The dominant use of the soft lavender colour on stripped floorboards, as well as on walls, bath, and toilet, creates a cocoon-like atmosphere and holds together any disparate elements Nowadays, with the improved heating of modern housing, the bathroom is a often one of the few havens of peace an tranquility in a home. It is good to remember this when you are planning what to include .

Above: this bathroom shouts privacy and relaxation. A stand-alone bath combined with low-level lighting adds to the feelings of tranquility and luxuriousness.

With such a wide range of antique furnishings available, bathrooms can be as quirky as you like and can evoke all kinds of periods. There are traditional roll-top baths, baths with shower canopies, baths with huge shower roses, slimline Art Deco baths, even wooden baths. Team them with a few other well-chosen antiques and you have a room with a timeless edge.

The moody and sensuous atmosphere of the bathroom above is created by the harmonious use of a single colour for the walls and floor and the low-level lighting, combined with an idiosyncratic bead curtain.

The bathtub featured opposite is probably from the Victorian era. It shouts "antique" with its gorgeous patina of age and subtle sheen, and its deep sides make it perfect for those who love a wallow.

***Above:** Atmospheric lighting and dramatic ferns create a theatrical feel to bathtime – especially when teamed with a deep, copper bath.*

The shine of the metal is cleverly echoed in two chunky Edwardian radiators, stripped of paint, that have been reconditioned to pump out heat.

The whole scheme has a fin de siècle feel to it, especially with the addition of several tall parlour palms, ubiquitous in late 19th-century and a sign of financial status and horticultural knowledge. Ambient lighting dotted around the bathroom creates atmosphere, especially in the evening, and draws the eye to a pair of oval mirrors, set pleasingly either side of the window.

An upholstered chair provides a place to lay towels and clothes, but when not needed is draped with a decadent animal print fabric and feather boa. There's a footstool for beautifying feet or providing a perch for a visitor. This modern-day equivalent of a boudoir works beautifully.

BATHROOM ANTIQUES

Small, pretty storage pieces are ideal for the bathroom, where space is often tight. Neo-classical designs – whether late 18th- and early 19th-century originals, or late 19th-century revival pieces – often have marble tops, which are practical as their surfaces are likely to get wet and wood alternatives mark all too easily. The marble also makes for a more attractive finish than modern-day plastics and is perfect for the display of vintage shaving and vanity sets. Clean and simple geometric forms suit the fresh feeling that many of us seek in our bathrooms – think bevelled mirrors and faceted Art Deco opaline glass jars. Alternatively, soft-coloured Venetian glass or the fluid forms of Art Nouveau ceramics create a gentler atmosphere for relaxation and contemplation.

***Below:** The elegant form and delicate blue of these 1950s-60s Murano glass bottles make them a perfect addition to a bathroom. The avventurine copper leaf inclusions add an sparkle reminiscent of light reflecting off the sea.*

***Left:** Lighting can continue a marine theme, such as this 1920s Art Deco wall light with its clam shell shade.*

***Below:** The presence of a bathing lady in this 1930s German pressed glass 'Muschel' (shell) soap dish by Walther makes it more desirable.*

BETTER TO BUY OLD THAN NEW

Vintage advertising or packaging, especially for washing products, or showing seaside or beach themes, offers better value for money than modern reproductions. As it is widely collected, if you decide to part with a piece, you will be able to cash in on your investment if you chose wisely. Posters can be more affordable than modern limited edition prints, but make sure valuable examples are framed professionally. This stylish tourist poster for the French Riviera, designed by Paolo Garetto in 1933, captures the romance of a message in a bottle.

Left: Acting as stylish storage for towels and other bathing accessories, the well-carved decoration on these French Louis XVI-style commodes adds value. Richly veined marble was typically used for the tops of washstands.

FOCUS ON: MAXIMALISM

Collecting antiques is a nationwide habit and it's catching. It usually starts out small and then snowballs into a quest that leads to visits to antiques fairs, shops, and garage sales whenever they crop up. Must-have pieces are pursued with relish, and knowledge about a subject grows with the collection. Once your hoard has been established, it's nice to show it off and, enjoy it.

The trouble with collections is that they often end up in drawers and boxes or hidden from view in a corner attracting dust. Instead, using finds to decorate a room can add to your home's sense of individuality and help emulate a period style that you particularly like. To start with, think of ways of incorporating your collection within existing furniture. You could, for example, make space for small items in a bookcase, to break the line of books and add interest; or put a glass or ceramic piece under a glass-topped lamp table.

If your collection is colourful, consider it as part of your decorating palette. Shelves filled with coloured glass or ceramics can look great against a white wall, for example, and you can position one or two star pieces to pick up key colours in fabrics and upholstery. This repetition of colour is pleasing to the eye and helps bring a feeling of consistency to a room scheme. Or be more restrained, with just one or two colourful things on a tabletop. Textiles lend themselves to display and look glorious hanging on the rungs of a bamboo ladder propped against the wall, or draped in woven baskets dotted about a room.

As an alternative to patterned wallpaper on your walls, use a collection to

A collection of vintage hats, shoes and buckles makes a dramatic centrepiece and sartorial statement in this room.

FASHION AS ART

Rather than storing vintage finds in a wardrobe, put them on show. You will find that a low occasional table is an ideal base to pile up bags and hats in a spiral pattern. Hang up special pieces, such as a dress or jacket, flat against the wall; stack hats on a milliner's hat block or stone bust; and put tiny things, such as children's clothing, in picture frames. Arrange shoes quirkily on floating shelves or, if they're really sculptural, place them at floor level.

Above: Kitsch collections suit the more-is-more approach to display. Here religious artefacts and souvenirs create a shrine to the owner's personal taste.

create vibrancy and interest. Arrange hotspots of paintings, prints, posters, and mirrors to catch the eye. Antique and vintage jewellery can look gorgeous pinned onto an old-fashioned tailor's dummy – the pieces are centre stage, and the collection becomes a talking point for anyone visiting. Pleasingly shaped hatboxes and woven-lidded boxes are ideal for keeping precious things free of dust but close to hand, to take out and enjoy.

OTHER ROOMS

Opposite: *A cosy corner with a comfortable chair and antique table is the perfect spot for catching up with correspondence or reading. The collection of objects also resembles a 'cabinet of curiosities', representing the owner's memories and travels around the world.*

As more of us work from home, a dedicated study or an area where we can plug in the laptop without being disturbed is becoming vital. As a result there's a renewed interest in desks and writing tables – pieces of furniture that were commonplace in many homes until the 1960s, but went out of favour with open-plan living and a more informal lifestyle.

An antique desk or bureau is likely to be far sturdier, made of better-quality wood, and more finely finished than anything that can be bought today, as the desk pictured shows. Laptops can be hidden brilliantly inside a bureau. Old desks often have decorative details that make the whole piece stand out, such as hand-carved panelling, reeded and balustered legs, and marquetry – the intricate art of making pattern with wooden inlays. There is a huge range of antique chairs to choose from, but try them out for comfort and height before you buy them, taking the dimensions of your desk with you when you go shopping. Interestingly, antique seats can often be wider than today's designs, because they were designed to accommodate a woman's full skirts. And extra space can mean extra comfort.

And if you'd rather keep any technology as low key as possible, divert the eye with a collection of antique prints hung over the desk. Combine different types of frame for maximum visual interest. A desk is also a place where a small collection can be displayed, some ceramics, wooden boxes – anything that takes your fancy. But remember, you still have to work in this space, so keep thinking that less is more so that you maintain the practicality of the space.

HALLWAY

Above: The graceful lines of this modern steel and wood spiral staircase are complemented by the solitary wooden dining chair, perfectly demonstrating how pieces from different periods can live together harmoniously.

Right: Storage furniture is vital in the hallway of a busy family home - where else do you keep hats, gloves, spare keys and the dog's lead?

As a room for displaying antiques, the entrance hall is often overlooked, yet arriving in a house that is immediately warm and welcoming can make all the difference to our mood.

An entrance hall is a great place to show off odds and ends that are hard to modernist hallway above shows one such example, where a one-off chair adds a homely touch to the clean lines of the chrome and wood spiral staircase and mellow parquet flooring.

In the hallway pictured opposite, a marble bust and a much loved plate enjoy pride of place on the brass-handled sideboard.The framed botanical prints add a sophisticated touch and tone in with the subtly patterned wallpaper. Illuminated by an elegant table lamp in the evenings, this hallway will provide a warm welcome for every visitor.

There are plenty of other options, too – a jaunty Victorian hat stand covered in a colourful jumble of coats, hats, and scarves; a collection of umbrellas and canes kept in a Chinese cylinder vase, for example.

This is an opportunity to think inventively and practically.A chair makes an ideal place for hanging scarves and bags; an old Singer sewing machine table can transform into a narrow console; and an antique terra-cotta pot will hold umbrellas and canes. Be bold and express your individuality.

The hallway is an often overlooked space, yet the note struck here sets the tone for the rest of the house.

FOCUS ON: DISPLAYING PICTURES

Paintings, prints, and photographs bring a room to life and add another layer of depth and personality to a home. As a general rule, large canvases look better hung in a large room, although they will add dramatic impact if they dominate the walls of a smaller room.

Smaller, single artworks suit corridors, stairwells, and corners. Hung alone in large rooms, they can appear lost, so group them with other prints or paintings for greater impact. Arranging odd numbers of artworks on a wall will encourage the eye to travel and rest on each one rather than sweeping over them too quickly.

Highly detailed and colourful artworks look best hung against a neutral background or a shade that is not overpowering. Treated this way, they will make great focal points. If a painting looks out of place, it may be that it is fighting with the decorating scheme – find somewhere calmer to hang it.

For a pleasing result when hanging a large painting or print, the centre of the artwork should be at eye level to be appreciated properly. When grouping smaller pictures, try to keep similar mediums together for consistency.

If artworks are the same size, create a bold look by hanging them symmetrically – cover a whole wall as opposite. If they vary in size, don't try to restrain them, but hang them asymmetrically to break the sightline and capitalize on their difference.

***Opposite:** A wall covered with a symmetrical display of photographs is an eye-catching way to remember friends and family.*

A varied collection of portraits arranged in a haphazard formation creates a homely, family display.

MIX IT UP

When planning an interior scheme it can be tempting to hang paintings, prints, and photographs in regimented ways so they look neat and symmetrical. However, doing the opposite can be at least as effective and brings a more homespun flavour. Artworks, especially when different genres, types or media, when arranged in an asymmetrical way are attractive because nature is haphazard and we are hard-wired into an innate love of natural forms. The visual benefit of a less restrained arrangement is that it creates a charming feel, like putting patchwork on walls.

CORRIDORS

Above: Practical flooring and traditional furniture draw visitors into the home. Ladderback chairs were made from the mid 18th century into the late 19th century. Look for signs of wear and a warm patina that has built up over centuries.

Most homes have a lot of corridor space that is largely ignored and not even taken into consideration when deciding where to display or store collections of antiques. But with a bit of imagination and design they can become mini galleries for things that won't fit elsewhere. Even the slimmest of spaces can be made special by placing china figurines or silverware on windowsills, or using a slender console table or chest to provide an extra display surface and storage. The additional wall space provided by corridors is another important consideration. When the main living room walls are full you can turn the corridors into a personal art gallery of prints, paintings, maps, mirrors, fans, framed textiles, samplers, wall hangings, tiles, or other two-dimensional treasures that take your fancy. And don't forget to utilize the handy space over doors.

Above: *Corridors are ideal places to show off personal collections. Use large paintings to create drama.*

The two or three large frames in the corridor shown above work well against the large expanse of neutrally coloured wall. But if you have lots of smaller collectables, such as hand mirrors or portrait miniatures or hats, group them together to give your collection visual impact.

The corners of corridors provide ideal spaces in which to display narrow antique furniture such as fire screens, bookcases, barometers, drop-leaf tables and stools.Then there are the floors, of course, which are the perfect backdrop for richly coloured antique rugs and runners.

Remember how you use the corridor in question. If it is between the kitchen and dining room, for example, try to incorporate a heatproof surface, such as a marble topped table, on which you can rest hot dishes when serving dinner.

FLOORING

If you are lucky enough to inherit an original floor, such as the tiles shown in the hallway opposite, it is wise to adjust your room décor to the look of the flooring as it would be a crying shame not to show off such a fabulous period feature to best advantage.

However, if you are adding a new floor from scratch (such as the more modern tiling scheme shown in the box below), there are a number of things you will need to take into account when choosing a flooring style. You need to think first about the practicalities. How hard wearing does your flooring need to be? Is the room subject to damp or condensation? Do you want a contemporary or a more historical look and feel? Do you have to think about whether noise will carry when the floor is walked upon? Does it need to be resilient to grease and other sources of staining? And finally, but perhaps most importantly, how much do you want to spend? There is an enormous variety of flooring available at both ends of the market. From vinyl and linoleum, to stone slabs, laminate flooring and all kinds of ceramic or terracotta tiles, the possibilities are endless. Certain flooring styles (such as the tiles in the hall shown opposite) date a room's décor immediately but this doesn't mean that they cannot also be used in a more contemporary home.

Opposite: *The traditional tiling in the hallway pictured opposite provides a warm welcome to visitors and is also practical and easy to clean. The period feel has been echoed sensitively in the carpet treatment and dado rail employed in the stairwell.*

The drama of the contemporary tiling in the hallway above is combined with cool white walls and modern sculpture.

THE FLOOR SHOW

Like a good pair of shoes, the perfect choice of flooring can add the finishing touch to the rest of your colour scheme. You need to chose a style that fits in with both your lifestyle and any period features already in your home, but that doesn't mean that you have to play safe. Strong colours and bold patterns, such as the geometric lines of the flooring in the image left, can be used to set off prized pieces of furniture or artworks, but be careful to add neutral walls and calming features to avoid the space feeling too cluttered.

BUYING ANTIQUES

BUYING ANTIQUES

Previous pages: *A selection of early 20th century handpainted and transfer-printed trio sets. Often costing only a few pounds each, a harlequin set adds interest to tea time.*

Buying antiques can become a serious habit! There are several ways in which you can go about it, the most obvious being to buy from antique dealers, from auction houses, or from the Internet (see Resources, p186). It may seem daunting to start with – not least because there is so much in-the-know terminology to get to grips with – but everyone has to begin somewhere, and it really does not take long for the amateur to build specialist knowledge. Whether you like the idea of having an eclectic mix of antiques in your house, or prefer to specialize in one or two styles it is paramount that you do some proper research into what to look for. While this chapter offers useful pointers to get you started, you should read books on the areas that interest you. Do not trust everything that you read though, especially on the internet – properly researched reference books are the most reliable way to build a lifetime of knowledge. In time you will be spotting typical examples at a glance as well as identifying the rarer pieces. You will also learn about the pitfalls you might encounter along the way. The sheer range and volume of available antiques makes it difficult to know where to start. The choice narrows down significantly, however, when you begin to think about what kind of antiques you want, which rooms they are for, what style or period you like, and how much money you have to spend. Whatever period you are looking at, there will be pieces made by well-known designers as well as generic examples of a similar style. It goes without saying that the former are almost always more expensive than the latter (but they will hold their value, while generic pieces may not). It is also worth bearing in mind that fashion has much to do with the price of an antique. With current interest in pieces from the mid-20th century, these are becoming increasingly difficult to find at fairs, and you may well pay over the odds from a dealer. On the other hand, Georgian, Victorian and Edwardian pieces are currently less desirable and can be bought at incredibly low prices.

TOP TIPS WHEN BUYING

- LEARN THE LINGO. Dealers and auction houses use phrases and terms with which you might be unfamiliar. Read books or ask to find out what they mean.
- SPEND THE MONEY. Buy the most expensive piece in its range that you can afford. The more desirable the piece, the more likely it is to hold its value.
- NEGOTIATE. All dealers are prepared to negotiate, but always be polite. You should always get a better deal for cash.
- GET A RECEIPT. Always ask for one, containing a description of the piece and any further information, such as date and provenance.
- LOOK FOR SIGNS OF QUALITY. Look for great craftsmanship, the best quality materials and design.

This striking 1970s Whitefriars Tangerine 'Banjo' vase, designed by Geoffrey Baxter in 1966, is typical of period style.

Opposite, top: *The fine craftsmanship of many antiques is hard to beat compared to modern examples. This Georgian silver teapot was made and decorated by hand.*

Opposite, bottom: *Deemed out of fashion, the mid–19th century German Biedermeier style of this dressing chest combines clean-lined, almost modern forms with a traditional Classical and architectural look.*

Be sure to take a good look at a piece before buying it. Examine all aspects of it so that you know exactly what condition it is in. Note any obvious damage and ask the seller as many questions as you like. There is nothing worse than getting a piece home only to realize that it has a chip, flaw, or scratch that you did not notice. And while many issues can be resolved, the cost of doing so may exceed the value of the piece.

Right: *Read books to get to grips with scarce or desirable patterns, forms and makers. This Art Deco Clarice Cliff 'Stamford' shape teaset is decorated with the rare and sought-after 'Mountain' pattern from 1932.*

BUYING FURNITURE: CHAIRS

Right: Wicker furniture, such as this Dryad chair, need not be confined to the garden or conservatory. Soften seats with a cushion. Vintage Lloyd Loom chairs, which are similar in look, are made with paper covered wire and can be found for less than new examples.

Broadly speaking, the better condition a chair is in, the more valuable it will be; pieces by known designers are usually worth more than generic versions; and chairs that bear typical characteristics of a period style are more desirable than those that do not. When buying chairs, therefore, it is useful to be able to identify them. Always consider the true date of an early piece. Chairs made pre-1700 should have stretchers between the legs. After this, corner blocks in seat frames resulted in stronger structures, meaning that stretchers were no longer necessary. The lack of stretchers made way for shaped legs – typically, the Rococo cabriole leg (early 18th century); the straight, tapering leg (late 18th century); and the sabre leg (early 19th century). All of these forms were revived from the mid- to late 19th century onwards, and careful checking of quality and wear should help distinguish an original from a revival piece.

Upholstery was rare in chairs until the early 18th century – it was largely restricted to pads on seats and chair backs and, sometimes, arms. The first true sofas and chaises longues date to the early 19th-century invention of sprung seating, while deep-padded button-back upholstery did not appear until the mid-19th century. Look for features that help identify the period style of an early piece, such as the wood from which it is made. Most chairs were made from oak until around 1700. After this they were made from walnut and, later, mahogany, often as veneers rather than solid wood. Do note any carving, veneering, marquetry, gilding, and so on, as well as the dominant decorative features (such as Rococo scrollwork or Neo-classical guilloches). Chairs

Below: The bold, sweeping curves of the back rail, legs and sides of this Regency rosewood chaise longue, c1820, make it as sculptural as it is desirable.

GET THE LOOK FOR LESS

Sets of identical chairs rise in price with the number of chairs in the set and with the age. This is because it becomes increasingly difficult to keep an original set intact as time goes by. For example, a set of 12 might be split as part of an inheritance, or several chairs could fall victim to fire or flood. If you are on a budget, consider buying a "harlequin" set – such as two sets of three identical chairs that work together but cost significantly less.

Three 'harlequin' Victorian balloon back chairs, c1865. The carved backs and back rails differ, even though the overall form is similar.

from the 20th century are often identifiable through stylistic features typical of the period (Art Nouveau and Art Deco, for example) and through the use of new materials – tubular steel in the 1930s, fibreglass, bent plywood, or foam upholstery in the 1950s, and revolutionary plastics in the 1960s and 1970s. Whether buying chairs at auction, from an antiques shop, or at a fair, make sure that you examine them carefully. For wooden chairs, check that the basic structure is sound and that there are no loose joints or signs of woodworm. If a chair is said to have its original upholstery, are the condition, style, and fibre of the fabric in keeping with its age? Check plastics and metals for areas of damage that there may be to the finish and discolouration.

Left: *This Mid–century Modern Form International set is based on Eero Saarinen's 1956 'Tulip' design, which aimed to "clear up the slum of legs" on chairs and tables in homes.*

CLEANING AND CARING FOR WOOD

All wooden furniture has an oil, wax, or French-polished finish, which, having built up over many years, gives furniture its patina and adds to its durability. If your pieces are in good condition and are looked after on a regular basis, they will not need too much maintenance. It may mean dusting them along with regular housework and re-applying the finish once or twice a year.

Most of the furniture you own is likely to have a wax or oil finish. You may have the odd French-polished piece – usually mahogany or walnut – which can be identified by its highly mirrored surfaces. In general terms, almost all oak and pine furniture sold in Britain today has a wax finish, while oil might be used on teak and other African hardwoods. Both finishes are easy to apply and involve wiping clear beeswax or boiled linseed oil onto the surface of the piece (sparingly in the case of wax and liberally in the case of oil) and buffing the surface to achieve a sheen. You can apply a number of coats to achieve the finish you want. French polishing takes some time to master, so you should seek professional advice here.

REPAIRING A SCRATCH

You can usually repair a scratch on a piece of furniture that has an oiled or waxed finish by wiping over the area with a shoe polish that matches the colour of the wood, and buffing it to blend it in. In French-polished pieces, the process is more complicated. The piece may have a final coat of beeswax, which needs to be removed before you attend to the scratch. To do this, simply wipe back and forth over the area with a little white spirit. Then start the repair by building up layers of French polish over the scratched area, allowing each layer to dry thoroughly between applications. Once you have enough layers that the polish stands proud of the surface, use the blunt edge of a scalpel to scrape it back, very carefully, until it is flush. Finally, apply a thin coat of beeswax polish to the entire surface.

It is surprisingly easy to elminate small scratches from furniture but if you are all concerned, remember it always pays to consult an expert.

It could be a good idea to revive your wooden furniture every other year using a commercial cleaning solution, which will restore its vibrancy and richness of colour. This is usually applied with a clean lint-free cloth (old cotton sheets are good for this). On pieces that are abnormally dirty – after storage in an attic or garage for several years – use a piece of extra-fine (grade 000) steel wool to apply the solution to begin with, working in the direction of the grain. After reviving a piece, always apply a coat of the appropriate finish to restore the natural patina.

You can maintain the patina of your wooden furniture for longer if you take a number of precautions when caring for it. Never put hot plates or cups on a wooden surface, as the heat may damage the finish. Keep pieces out of direct sunlight, which tends to bleach wood surfaces. Always clear up spills as soon as possible to prevent them from getting under the finish of the piece and into the grain of the wood.

***Above:** This elegant yet practical Neoclassical Georgian demi-lune table is made from satinwood and mahogany, with boxwood and ebony inlay.*

***Left:** In the past, hall chairs such as this Victorian mahogany example, were not designed for comfort but as practical seats for visiting tradesmen. The better the carving, the higher the price.*

***Far left:** Inspired by the great Georgian designer Thomas Sheraton, this Edwardian dressing table has inlaid rosewood and ebony on a satinwood veneer. Quality such as this is hard to come by, in today's furniture.*

CLEANING AND CARING FOR UPHOLSTERY

Opposite, below left: *The condition of the gold velvet on this sturdy 19th century throne armchair takes the concept of 'shabby chic' to its limits, or makes it an ideal candidate for recovering.*

Opposite, below right: *Although not to everyone's tastes, the detailed original gros and petit point needlework on this 19th century wing armchair add desirability and value. Unless badly damaged, do not consider re–upholstery.*

Over time, upholstered furniture needs cleaning, particularly armchairs and sofas, which take an incredible amount of use – spills, stains, and scuffs are inevitable. While the majority of modern-day fabrics have all manner of protective, soil-resistant coatings, this is not the case with vintage or antique pieces.

For any piece of upholstered furniture of reasonable value, the best advice is to have it cleaned professionally. For pieces of lesser value, you could undertake the cleaning yourself. Commercial products for general cleaning are widely available, and it is usually a question of choosing the right one for the kind of fabric you have (cotton, linen, wool) and testing an inconspicuous area for colourfastness before proceeding. There are numerous ways in which to deal with obvious, identifiable stains and a good book on household cleaning will list them. In all cases it is imperative that spills and stains are dealt with as soon as possible and that any application of a recommended solution is sparing and gentle.

Leather upholstery dries out over time and can flake or crack, so it is a good idea to "feed" your leather furniture once in a while in order to maintain its suppleness. Commercial products are available for this and are usually rubbed into the surface of the leather with a clean cloth. While marks are undesirable on most types of upholstery, this is not always the case with leather. Instead, stains, scuffs, and scratches mellow over time and contribute to the patina of a piece. It is wise, therefore, not to attempt to clean leather too rigorously. For a general clean, saddle soap is the best method, applied as a lather with a damp sponge and removed using an almost dry sponge before patting dry.

You can prolong the life expectancy of your upholstery by looking after it well and vacuuming it regularly. Fabrics and leather surfaces bleach in direct sunlight, so bear this in mind when positioning a piece of furniture. Upholstered furniture also suffers in damp or humid rooms and can become mouldy, so try to keep rooms well ventilated.

Below: *Designed in 1950 by Danish designer Hans Wegner, this teak and orange wool upholstered 'Papa Bear' armchair updates the comfortable Georgian wing armchair for a new century.*

VINTAGE CLASSICS

Leather chairs have become fashionable statement pieces in a room, making a more interesting alternative to matching chairs from the ubiquitous three-piece suite. Whilst new examples can be found to do the job, vintage examples from the late 19th century onwards can make a better investment. As they have offered decades of comfort, many will be worn – do not be put off as a battered, loved appearance appeals to fans of the shabby chic look, and is to be expected. However, beware of badly torn leather that could be difficult to re-stitch, dry and cracked leather, or a badly sprung structure or frame. Currently, those in 1920s-1930s Art Deco forms, or those that are typical of 1960s-1970s styles, are the most popular. Often a coat of leather cream will work wonders – leather is one of the only forms of upholstery that improves with age.

This leather arm chair, c1900, is based on designs from the 1840s. The turned mahogany legs and lyre-shaped arms are desirable.

BUYING FURNITURE: TABLES

Over the years, tables have been designed to suit a wide range of functions. Dining tables exist in all manner of shapes, sizes, and materials, and there are countless games tables, dressing tables, occasional tables, and tea and coffee tables to choose from. In very general terms, the more typical a piece is for its period, the more desirable it is likely to be. Relative rarity, quality of craftsmanship, and provenance add to the value of a piece.

As with any antique, a thorough examination of a piece is essential before buying in order to establish that it is genuine. There are several areas to consider. First, is the form of the table correct for its period? Tables underwent a similar evolution to chairs (see p.66), with a move from stretchers to cabriole legs to straight tapering legs from the early 18th century to the mid-19th century. The same primary timbers were also fashionable – oak (pre-1700), walnut (1700–1760), and mahogany (1760 onward). Dining tables tended to have solid tops until the late 19th century. But there are countless forms, and it is important to know, roughly, when they first date from. For example, small drop-leaf Pembroke tables were rare before the 1750s; sofa tables are typically post-1800; extended dining tables did not exist before the 19th century; and the coffee table did not emerge until after World War II. Tables from the 20th century often have glass, plastic, or metal elements, which help to establish the date or period to which they belong.

Before buying, always check wooden tables for loose joints, chipped veneers, deep scratches, and woodworm. Some areas of damage – burns and ink spills, for example – tend to add to the patina of a piece, but they are always worth noting. If looking at a table with removable or drop leaves, check that they are all of the same wood and are a consistent colour. Some areas may be bleached, having been exposed to sunlight more often. Finally, consider the practicality of a table for its purpose. A French-polish finish is not ideal for dining or dressing tables that get a lot of use, as it scratches easily and is easily damaged by spills, while stretchers on tables interfere with leg room.

***Below:** The use of brightly coloured circles, metal tubes and ball feet on this 1950s table by Greta Magnusson Grossman for Glenn of California recall atomic and scientific models, which were an inspiration to many 1950s designers.*

A CRITICAL EYE

It is not unusual for tables to have been modified, and this could affect the value, authenticity, and practicality of a piece. For example, not all tabletops are on their original bases. Look at the underside of a table for any inexplicable holes where other legs may have been fitted. Also, tabletops are sometimes trimmed to make them smaller or a different shape according to changing fashion. Always consider the proportion and size, and look for dirty finger marks on the outside edge of the underside. Damaged feet of older, rustic tables may have been shortened, making the table shorter and no longer comfortable to sit at.

Right: *18th and 19th century sofa or 'Pembroke' tables have folding tops. When folded down, their compact form makes them ideal for smaller rooms. This Regency rosewood example, c1810, has unusual square section tapered cabriole legs and cross–banded kingwood inlay, which both add value.*

Right: *Placed beside a sofa or chair, tilt-top tripod tables are a practical solution for cups, glasses or lamps. This George III mahogany table has a desirable 'pie–crust' top and well carved acanthus leaf decoration on the legs.*

Far right: *Furniture designed for specific purposes can still be practical today. The angled top, folding leaves and many drawers of this early 19th century rosewood work table are as useful today as they were nearly two centuries ago.*

LIGHTING

There are so many options when planning lighting it's like contemplating an old fashioned sweetshop. There are wall lights and ceiling lights, spotlights and lamps, carriage lights for outdoors and solar lights for lining paths in myriad styles. Choosing lighting shouldn't be rushed as the right combination contributes hugely to the overall atmosphere of a home. And be eclectic, it's more interesting to have a range of styles dotted through rooms than just one look.

The purpose of lighting is split into three distinct categories. Ambient lighting provides overall illumination and is provided by ceiling pendants, ceiling spotlights and uplighters. Next comes task lighting such as floor lamps, table lamps, under cabinet fixtures, and adjustable ceiling lamps – over a dining room table for example. The final genre is accent lighting, usually spotlights or downlighters that throw a direct beam of light on something special. The main living areas are the rooms that will benefit from a mixture of all three categories of lighting. Globe or enclosed pendant lights are best for diffusing light

LIGHT FANTASTIC

Just as a glowing fire in a grate magnetises our attention so does a beautiful, sculptural light. As technology develops lighting design becomes more adventurous, giving us light sculptures and artworks, and highly contemporary chandeliers. A big and bold statement or an investment piece needs to be given space around it, so if it is floor based draw it away from the walls and cut down clutter around it. Hung from the ceiling, a quirky modern chandelier, or even a group of different yet similar shades as here, will hold a room from top down.

Three similar 1930s-50s French moulded frosted glass plafonniers.

Above: Sometimes, the most casual of lighting schemes can add drama and atmosphere. The simple rope lights in the room above transform a room into a seductive paradise after dark.

around a sitting room, while open shades pool the light downwards. For glamour it's hard to beat a chandelier, but not if it's the main source of ambient light. Task lighting is especially useful in the kitchen close to worktops, while spots over a kitchen range, a bookshelf or dresser highlight the decorative elements of a predominately utilitarian space.

When harsh ambient lighting is not required, floor and table lamps create a welcoming atmosphere. In the evenings the soft light of an arching floor lamp enables reading and close work, while table lamps placed underneath special paintings will cast a lovely glow onto the wall. Standard lamps have been popular since the 1930s and make a nostalgic statement, even when the design has been given a modern makeover.

Lighting can be used very effectively to highlight collections. Install spotlights to illuminate shelving arranged with glass and ceramics, or direct a beam onto a special large piece such as a vase or small piece of furniture. Collections arranged on wall space, from textiles to prints to books, become focal points under subtle spotlighting.

FOCUS ON: ERCOL FURNITURE

Above: The room shown in this 1960s advertisement for Ercol is typical of the 'Contemporary' style of the 1950s & 60s. Simple, modern lines are combined with bright colours in a minimal environment.

The mainstay of many a middle-class home during the 1960s and 1970s, Ercol is the epitome of high-quality, handmade British furniture. Made from solid beech, elm, or ash, the designs are simple and unembellished, relying principally on the beauty of the natural wood for their success.

The company was founded in High Wycombe, Buckinghamshire, in 1920 by Lucian Ercolani and it continues to flourish to this day. Working with the latest steam-bending processes he created a number of chair and table designs, of which perhaps the best known is his take on the hoop-back Windsor chair that originated in the area in the late 17th century, and which he showed at the influential "Britain Can Make It" exhibition of 1946. With three chairs being made every minute, this was the world's first mass-produced Windsor chair.

Despite the fact that Ercol furniture is often considered traditional, it was modern and shared many characteristics with the hugely successful Scandinavian design that dominated the post-war years, including traditional craftsmanship, soft rounded forms, and natural woods. Much of Ercol's success in the post-war decades can be attributed to this, and given the current revival of interest in Scandinavian mid-century furniture, it stands to reason see that Ercol is making something of a comeback.

With other British firms of the period becoming more sought after in recent years – such as G Plan and Stag, known for their modern-style quality wooden furniture at affordable prices – there is obviously an interest in good British design. Indeed, the influential fashion icon Margaret Howell has re-introduced Ercol furniture as a design classic in her prestigious boutiques. More vintage design dealers are following her lead, forcing both demand and value to rise.

The advantage of buying Ercol now is that there is plenty of it about and it is relatively cheap. Furthermore, you can currently buy pieces for far less than the equivalent Scandinavian pieces, thereby achieving that Mid-century Modern look without compromising on quality. Look for pieces that are made from light-coloured woods – more versatile than darker woods, as they go with any interior design scheme – and that bear typical Mid-century Modern furniture characteristics: Windsor-type forms with elegant turned spindles, and tables (dining, coffee, or nests of) with rounded corners and splayed turned legs.

Above: *Ercol's 'Love Seat' is an extension of the traditional Windsor chair range and, seating two comfortably, can be used either as a stand-alone piece or as a two-person bench with a dining table.*

Left: *Released in 1958 with a curved, laminated wood back and seat, the 'Butterfly' chair is a British take on the iconic 'DCW' plywood chair, designed by Charles and Ray Eames in 1945.*

VINTAGE CLASSICS

Designed in 1956 (and still available today as part of the "Ercol Originals" collection), this nest of three tables perfectly represents what is most appealing about Ercol's designs following World War II. The gently curving shape of the tabletops and the tapered legs are typical of 1950s/1960s organic, sculptural designs. Very much in vogue today, these tables - affectionately called "pebble tables" by collectors – can be found for under £150 for a set at antique fairs or in online auctions, a bargain for those who hunt for long enough. Always aim to buy light wood examples, as dark wood versions are not at all as desirable or valuable.

BUYING FURNITURE: STORAGE

Fitted kitchens, alcove shelving, and built-in wardrobes, all familiar features of the modern home, have done much to reduce the popularity of free-standing storage furniture in recent years. As a result, vintage pieces are among the best-value antique furniture you can buy. From wardrobes and chests of drawers to cupboards, sideboards, and dressers, good-quality storage furniture is plentiful and easy to find at auctions and antiques fairs.

In determining the age and authenticity of a piece, it is important to know a little history. The linen press – essentially a large shelved cupboard – and the open-shelved dresser emerged during the 17th century. Chests of drawers were rare before the middle of the 18th century, having evolved from the slightly earlier two-drawer commode, while the late 18th century brought the fall-front desk. The sideboard, an early 18th-century form, underwent a revival in the years following World War II. The display cabinet, often glazed, was a mainstay of the Victorian era and subsequent Art Nouveau period.

Having established the form and likely date of a piece, double check by considering its design, looking at the type of wood used, whether it is carved or veneered, the shape of any cornices and pediments, and the type of legs or feet a piece has. Look closely at individual components – drawers and doors, for example – to see if they have been machine- or handmade (telltale signs of a later piece are precision and uniformity in the joints). Check handles and any other fittings, which may have been replaced with versions from a later piece. Look for makers' labels on later pieces.

As with antique tables (see p.72), it is not unusual to see modifications in certain pieces over the years. While this is not always undesirable, it could have an impact on the value of a piece, and you should make sure the price you pay reflects this. Tall bookcases may have had pediments removed to fit into rooms with lower ceilings; the top section of a linen press may have been adapted to take a hanging rail; decorative panels may have been taken from older pieces.

***Below:** Made from coloured Masonite panels on a steel frame, this functional ESU 201 storage unit designed c1952 for Herman Miller by Charles and Ray Eames fulfills perfectly their objective to arrange "elements in such a way as to best accomplish a particular purpose".*

A CRITICAL EYE

Storage pieces consisting of more than one component – typically chests on chests, bookcase cabinets, or chests on stands – may get separated over the years. In some cases, the top might end up for sale with the bottom part of a different piece from the same period, such as with the piece shown here. This is known as a "marriage" and should be reflected in the price. Always check that the wood/veneer and colour are consistent across both halves. Make sure that fittings (hinges and handles) match throughout the piece and that decorative features in both halves match identically.

Left: *By using walnut, Edward Wormley harks back to traditional antique chests of drawers with his 1950s version for Dunbar. However, the pared down, minimal form and integral, recessed handles are strictly Modernist in style.*

Right: *Original, period painted decoration is highly desirable, but the later, 20th century painted design on this George III serpentine fronted mahogany chest of drawers should be removed to reveal the beauty of the piece as intended by the cabinet maker.*

STORAGE SOLUTIONS

New homes often have smaller proportions than older houses, and coupled with lots of us choosing to adapt our homes rather than move, storage is vital to making the most of available space. Effective storage cuts down on clutter and allows good pieces of furniture, special ornaments, collections and artworks to shine out, not play second fiddle to "stuff".

To begin with consider what you already have that can be reutilized to maximize storage. Think laterally. An attractive single chair, for example, could happily become a shelf for books, or a stool a mini display table for collectables or a lamp. A desk makes a perfect dressing table, with a drawer to store make-up in and a shelf for perfumes and toiletries. While an unwanted bookcase can be stacked up with table linen, tea towels and soaps.

Antique furniture is surprisingly versatile when it comes to providing storage. Chests of all kinds – old luggage, tuck boxes, blanket boxes and wooden trunks are small enough not to be obtrusive within a room scheme, but deep enough to store plenty of bits and bobs, both in and on them – old photo albums, documents, nick-nacks, bed linen and small items of clothing. Trunks make great coffee tables, with plenty of space inside them as well. Wooden boxes can store keys, spare buttons and business cards. From contemporary ranges, faux leather and woven boxes look good with most styles of furniture and are handy for tidying away piles.

Below: A classic Ericsson Ericophone or 'Cobra' phone, designed in the early 1950s by Ralph Lysell and Gösta Thames, sits on a deep shelf that also contains a useful drawer. The geometric wallpaper continues the Modern theme.*

A wide range of sideboards and cabinets from the early and mid-20th century can be used traditionally in a dining area for cutlery, glasses and tablemats or reinvented in the bedroom and used for holding books, DVDs, make-up and perching the TV or radio on. Look for antique pieces that have extra drawers, shelves and compartments such as old-fashioned wash stands, plan chests, tool boxes, needlework tables and sheet music stools, all of which provide extra opportunities for hiding things away.

Think along modernist lines when planning storage. This ground breaking early 20th century design movement was the first to incorporate in-built storage into homes. Commissioning a carpenter to make some neat cupboards, wardrobes and alcove shelves that stretch up to the ceiling could really maximize your space.

MAKING GOOD USE OF AWKWARD SPACES

In every home there are forgotten corners that have potential for providing storage. Stairwells are typically awkward – narrow and twisty, but with a bit of ingenuity can accommodate some bespoke drawers or a desk installed into the void beneath them. Then there are those tricky spaces in between rooms and doorways – erect floor to ceiling shelving for an elegant solution; filled with books and collections the shelves will become part of the decorating scheme.

BUYING FURNITURE: BEDS

Once the most valued item of furniture in a home, a bed continues to be a relatively expensive item to buy. However, antique and vintage beds are well priced compared with modern beds (often due to an incompatibility of mattress size) and should always hold their value in the long term.

It is possible to find beds from all major periods of recent history – from Georgian mahogany four-posters or pretty French cast-iron examples from the mid- to late 19th century to huge Postmodern extravaganzas. Make sure they all display the right style features for their supposed age. For example, is a four-poster made from an appropriate wood for the period to which it is attributed (walnut for early Georgian, mahogany for late Georgian, oak for Arts and Crafts)? Is there any surface ornamentation? What shape is the bed? What kind of feet does it have? These questions should help to identify the period in which the bed was designed.

Beds were originally smaller than they are now, and some will have been altered in width and length to compensate for this. Look for evidence of a bed having been expanded to fit modern wider mattresses, or shortened in height (in the case of a four-poster) to fit rooms with lower ceilings. Carved elements may end abruptly, for example, they may have sections that are inferior in quality to others, or the proportions of a bed might seem wrong.

More than any other form of antique furniture, beds are likely to entail a host of hidden costs. For example, most cast-iron beds at fairs are sold as head and foot ends with side rails. It is up to you to get slats made for the bed and to order the right-size mattress. Bespoke mattresses are readily available but expensive. Similarly, you will not want the original Georgian mattress (even if it were still in existence), but you will need to make sure a Georgian four-poster has the right detail to support a modern equivalent. Many iron beds are sold in their original, often chipped, painted state. While this appeals to some, others prefer a more polished look, which will add considerably to the price. Ensure you have a tape measure as while most cast-iron beds from the mid- to late 19th century are standard double size – 137cm (4ft 6in), some are only 122cm (4ft) – a critical 15cm (6in) that is very difficult to discern by eye.

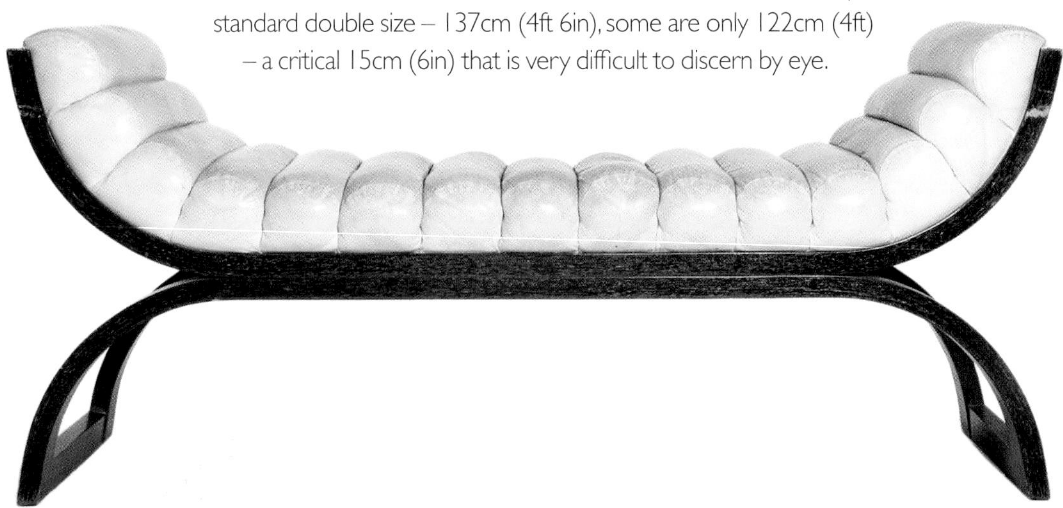

Below: *Although made in the 1950s, the shape of this Italian white leather upholstered ebonised oak daybed is strongly reminiscent of 18th century Neoclassical designs.*

BETTER TO BUY OLD THAN NEW

Developed in the Regency period, chaise longues were originally made in mirror image pairs, even though they are usually sold singly today. The quality of the decoration, be it carved or painted, and the elegance of the form are key to value. Solid wood antique versions, many from the Victorian era, can be found for £200-800 and can represent much better value than modern day versions. Always factor in upholstery costs when considering a purchase.

This early 20th century French Rococo–style chaise longue, priced at £850, has been re–upholstered to great effect.

Left: *Most Louis XV, Rococo-style, furniture found today dates from the 19th or early 20th centuries. The style and quality of the marquetry detail, and use of rosewood and gilt brass on this bed indicates a late 19th century origin.*

Below: *The heavy curving elements of this oak and steel bed are typical of Jonathan Singleton's current designs for Spain's SIG Furniture.*

BUYING CERAMICS: POTTERY

Right: This 18th century English Delftware pottery bowl is decorated with a colourful Chinoiserie scene that would have been very fashionable at the time.

In order to know what to look for when buying ceramics, you must first learn to distinguish between "pottery" and "porcelain". The easiest way to tell them apart is by the look, feel, and sound. Pottery (earthenware and stoneware) tends to be thicker, coarser, and heavier than porcelain. It is also often opaque, while porcelain is mostly translucent when held up to the light. If the side of a bowl or plate is tapped, porcelain will give a ringing sound as opposed to the hollow thud of earthenware. Chips in pottery have a rough, granular surface, while those in porcelain are crisp and smooth. Finally, porcelain tends to feel colder than pottery.

To check whether a piece of pottery is authentic, you need to decide whether it fulfils certain criteria. The most important are the type of glaze used (tin, lead), whether the design has been hand-painted or printed, the way in which colour was added (underglaze or overglaze), the style of the

Despite being charmingly naïve, this mid–19th century group is well painted and has plenty of detail compared to later reproductions.

A CRITICAL EYE

To compete with the leading porcelain factories of the day, the Staffordshire potteries began to produce large numbers of pottery figures from the beginning of the 19th century. Often depicting rural scenes, with trees and domestic animals, the figures proved hugely popular, and production continued well into the Victorian era. More modern reproductions are often found, and should be avoided if buying for investment. Early pieces tend to have more detail, and are usually better painted. Earlier gilt details tends to be warmer and more coppery in tone. Later copies are also lighter in weight.

decoration (Rococo, Neo-classical, and so on), and whether a piece bears a maker's mark (see Resources section p. 186 for a selection of examples).

In very general, delftware (tin-glazed earthenware with underglaze colour and a distinctive shiny, sometimes blue-tinged glaze) was made from the late 17th to the mid-18th century. Creamware (a cream-coloured earthenware with a lead glaze and either underglaze or overglaze colour) – and the slightly whiter pearlware, which became the preferred medium for the company's blue-and-white transfer-printed wares (see p.86) – were developed by the Staffordshire potteries, such as Spode and Wedgwood, from the mid- to late 18th century and continued to be made well into the 19th century. Unglazed stoneware created by Wedgwood became fashionable in the late 18th to mid-19th century.

There are patterns, colours, and decorative details associated with each of these types of ceramic – for example, chinoiserie in delftware, elaborate piercing in creamware, and archetypal Neo-classical forms in Wedgwood's unglazed stoneware.

Arts and Crafts pieces, and those from the Art Nouveau period, reflect a trend toward art and studio pottery that continues to this day. It includes high-quality, one-off pieces designed and handmade by craftsmen, many of them characterized by innovative, often matt glazes. With mass production, a new trend emerged, in which leading potteries, such as A.J. Wilkinson and, later, Midwinter, commissioned designers to create wares for an ever-growing middle-class market. Look for pieces that reflect the fashions of the day, notably those made in the Art Deco period and during the 1950s.

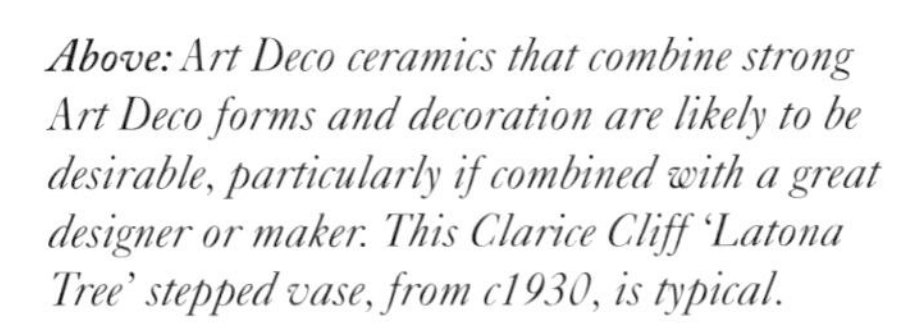

***Above:** Art Deco ceramics that combine strong Art Deco forms and decoration are likely to be desirable, particularly if combined with a great designer or maker. This Clarice Cliff 'Latona Tree' stepped vase, from c1930, is typical.*

***Right:** Black and white zebra stripes were highly fashionable in the 1950s, and similar designs were produced by a number of factories. Midwinter's 'Zambesi', designed by Jessie Tait in 1956, is the most famous and sought–after.*

FOCUS ON: BLUE-AND-WHITE CERAMICS

Right: *Although inspired by Chinese designs, the much–loved Willow pattern, and the story behind it, is an English invention. It was first used by Thomas Minton in 1780, but went on to be copied by many other factories, and is still produced today.*

Below: *The 'Asiatic Pheasants' pattern was produced for roughly a century from the 1830s onwards. Printed in a lighter blue, it became one of the most popular choices for Victorian dinnerware. Displaying the pattern very well, this large meat platter by Beech & Hancock offers excellent value for money.*

Mass-produced by the Staffordshire potteries from the mid-18th century onwards, blue-and-white ceramics were inspired by Chinese hand-painted blue-and-white porcelain. By transfer-printing their designs onto their wares, instead of painting them on, the potteries were able to reduce manufacturing costs, and they began to produce them on a much larger scale. Hugely successful well into the 19th century, they were exported all over the world.

Transfer printing was achieved by etching a design onto a copper plate, which was then heated slightly and coated in ink. Paper was pressed onto the copper plate to pick up the design, which was then transferred to a biscuit-fired plate, cup, bowl, or jug. Next, the piece was glazed and finally fired again.

Designs were often inspired by Chinese scenes, including the ubiquitous "Willow Pattern", but also by scenes of ancient Rome and Greece, in keeping with the prevailing Neo-classical style.

With current fashions favouring the clean lines of Mid-century Modern designs, many country styles have fallen out of favour and prices have plummeted. But there are many reasons why blue-and-white ceramics should make a comeback. A striking focal piece can work well in a minimalist interior, while a collection creates an instant 'country cottage' feel. Furthermore, these ceramics are hardwearing, plentiful, and practical, which makes them an attractive

GET THE LOOK FOR LESS

While a Victorian family may have used one or two tureens, they may have needed eight or more plates. This makes plates a more common, and as such more affordable, choice to buy today. The flat surface shows off the pattern very well, and a display of plates arranged on a wall or country pine or oak dresser creates enormous visual impact. Although a set of matching patterns looks stunning, feel free to mix patterns and sizes. As plates were used regularly, always check the edges for chips, and tap them to check for cracks. Avoid those that are stained, or have a network of fine lines known as crazing, as this is impossible to restore.

The selection of plates in different sizes and patterns above works harmoniously, even though they vary in country of origin from China to England, and in date from the 19th to 20th centuries.

purchase for the short term and a potential investment for the long term. When looking for pieces, bear in mind that the pattern and shape of a piece will count toward its desirability. The "Death of The Bear" pattern is worth more than the "Willow" pattern, for example, and baby feeders or tureens with spoons and dishes are worth much more than plates.

The value of rare and desirable shapes and patterns has remained strong. Particularly worth seeking out are the smudgy "Flow Blue" ceramics, hugely popular in the US. Generally much darker than the usual patterns, the style came about owing to a mistake during the manufacturing process, yet proved so popular on arrival in the US that the error had to be replicated on a mass scale. For novices, a small milk jug or plate sourced from a fair might be a good starting point and could cost well under £30.

***Below:** Spode is one of the most notable names in blue and white ceramics, and the company is still producing examples today. This footbath is decorated with the desirable 'Girl at the well' pattern, and dates from c1822.*

BUYING CERAMICS: PORCELAIN

There are two types of porcelain – hard paste and soft paste. The main difference between the two is the presence of china clay (kaolin) in hard-paste porcelain – soft-paste, a substitute for true porcelain, contains ground glass. Typically, hard-paste porcelain is translucent, the clear glaze having fused with the body during firing. Soft-paste porcelain is not translucent and is characterized by a glaze that is separate from the body of a piece.

Porcelain originated in China and became hugely popular in Europe from the 17th century onward – so much so that European factories scrambled to produce their own porcelain in order to satisfy growing demands. The many thousands of pieces available to antique buyers today include original Chinese wares, imitations of those pieces, forgeries of those pieces, and European wares inspired by those pieces. There are also countless European pieces designed in their own right in response to the ever-changing fashions of the day.

Below: Don't ignore 20th century porcelain, as it may be a wise investment for the future. Look for designs that are typical of the period they were made in, and notable names, such as this 'Modulation' coffee service designed in 1965 by the Finnish designer Tapio Wirkkala for Rosenthal of Germany.

It is important to learn to tell the difference between soft- and hard-paste porcelain, and the key lies in handling as many pieces as possible. Hard paste tends to be a brilliant white compared with the grey-white of soft paste. Hard paste is also much smoother in consistency, while soft paste tends to be more granular. These characteristics, along with the visible difference in glazes (see above), are the best way to tell the difference between the two.

In terms of dates, while Meissen had discovered hard-paste porcelain by 1710, Sèvres did not have it until 1769, so any French porcelain before this date must be soft paste. The success of Meissen and Sèvres lead to many imitators, all producing quality wares, typically in Rococo and Neo-classical styles of their day (see Know Your Style, p.140). Look for the superior quality of Meissen in terms of complexity of shape and precise decoration.

From around 1750, numerous factories in Britain began to produce porcelain, among them the Worcester, Derby, Coalport, and Staffordshire factories. Styles predominantly imitated French

A CRITICAL EYE

When it comes to dating ceramics, the style of the form and decoration can help but, as styles were often reproduced, look at marks on the base for confirmation. One rule of thumb is to see if the country of origin is given. If it is, this suggests it was made after 1891. The words "Made in" began to appear on pieces made after 1914. A royal coat of arms indicates a piece was made no earlier than 1800, but could be much later. The word "Royal" in a British firm's name dates from the late 19th or 20th centuries, and the words "Bone China" were only used in the 20th century.

A Paragon printed mark used from 1935 onwards, from the base of an Art Deco tea cup and saucer.

and German styles. Names to look out for include Barr, Flight & Barr, and Doulton. During the 20th century, as with the potteries, a trend developed for porcelain manufacturers to commission contemporary designers to create designs for their wares. When establishing authenticity, always check ceramics for signs of wear – small chips to the rim of a plate, for example, or any obvious restoration. Look also for cracks or defects in the glaze, such as crazing.

Above left: *Meissen's porcelain figurines are unparalleled in terms of their quality and detail. Pastoral characters, dancers and musicians, such as these 19th century Turkish Malabars, decorated the homes of the wealthy or aristocracy and are still widely collected today.*

Above right: *Eccentric and colourful Postmodern ceramics should rise in value as demand increases. This Italian Flavia 'Colorado' teapot, designed in 1983 by Marco Zanini for Memphis, is an excellent example.*

Below right: *The market for Chinese ceramics has grown enormously over the past five years. Decorated in the pink dominated 'famille rose' palette, this bowl dates from the 18th century.*

DISPLAYING CERAMICS

Ceramics are woven into the fabric of our lives – we use them every day and have done for centuries, and they continue to hold our fascination. Pieces range from simple and practical stoneware, to delicate and ornamental porcelain, to colourful earthenware. Plain, patterned, large and small, ceramics come in such a variety of styles and shapes that a collection can be as multi-faceted as you like and a delight to build up over the years.

Ceramics lend themselves extremely well to grouping, so keep like with like for strong visual appeal if placing on a highly visible shelf or purpose-built unit. Arrange them according to colour and/or shape. Bowls work particularly well arranged together on a deep windowsill, or wooden shelves in a living room, or ranged down the centre of a long dining table. Use them for fruit or pot pourri or simply leave them empty so you can admire the interior glazes. Practical jugs look great in a kitchen on shelves or a dresser – display according to type of ware or amass a particular size such as cream jugs.

Tea and coffee wares are timeless in their appeal and all have the same homely purpose – to revive the owner. Now it is often the decoration that revives – there is much mismatched Victorian and Edwardian floral china available at great prices. Hunt for odd side plates, coffee cans, milk jugs, or teapots, and display them in harlequin style as a charming assortment. Place a short row of teacups and saucers along a windowsill or make dainty towers of plates that

If you are lucky enough to own a dresser, display a collection of pretty china – and remember that it doesn't matter whether it matches or not,

MIX IT UP

With their curvaceous shapes and amazing range of colours, ceramics are naturally equipped for creating wow factor. A mantelpiece with a mirror behind is the ideal place to arrange a selection and doubles the impact with reflections. Choose pieces with height and girth to draw the eye upwards and along, putting one star piece in the middle as the focal point. A redundant fireplace (or the alcove to either side of it) is another potential showcase for a collection of large-scale ceramics contrasted in shape to occupy the space fully.

__Above:__ The straight lines and primary colours of Gerrit Rietveld's 1918 'Red and Blue Chair' are echoed in the rug. In turn, both echo Piet Mondrian's abstract paintings. The rounded forms and earthy textures of the Mid-century Modern Italian pottery on the hearth contrast with the geometricity of this interior.

can also be rushed into service if visitors descend. A selection of wares on a silver-plated tray makes for an eye-catching tablescape, while odd teacups can be turned into dainty containers for cufflinks, jewellery and safety pins.

Plates and platters can be used to decorate empty wall space, or propped up above a dresser. Also consider wall mounting "lost souls": lids that have lost their vessels, small sauce tureens without lids, and saucers without cups for an intriguing display. For something a bit different, display ornamental figurines under a clear glass cheese or cake dome.

CLEANING AND CARING FOR CERAMICS

Right: Always check ceramic figurines carefully for damage or repair. The hat, head, elbows and legs of this 1930s Goldscheider 'Austrian Country Girl', designed by Josef Lorenzl, can all be damaged when cleaned or moved.

Most ceramics fall into one of two categories – those that are used primarily for display, and those used more frequently for serving food and drink. The best way to care for those on display is to store them in a dry place and to dust them regularly. Pieces kept in display cabinets and cupboards need dusting less frequently than those exposed to the air. They also benefit from occasional cleaning, while ceramics that you use for serving food will need cleaning more often.

The methods you use when cleaning your ceramics will depend on how a piece has been made and whether it is glazed or not, as it is the glaze that makes it waterproof. In very general terms, the majority of porcelain is fully glazed, while most pottery pieces have an area that is not glazed – the base of a bowl or vase, for example, or, in the case of some earthenware and stoneware, entire pieces. For partially glazed or non-glazed pieces, the best cleaning method is to wipe the surface carefully with a barely damp cloth. Use soap for stubborn stains, but take care to remove all traces, before patting the piece dry with towelling. All glazed pieces can be washed using warm water and a mild detergent. It is good practice to rinse items used for serving food immediately after eating – even if you intend to wash them later – as this could reduce staining. For more valuable pieces, it pays to wash them one at a time, rinsing them in clean warm water and drying them immediately. At no point should you scrub or scour a piece and do not be tempted to put vintage ceramics in the dishwasher.

You can prolong the life of your ceramics by taking greater care of them. For pieces on display, use correct-sized stands and holders that are able to carry the weight and that will hold a piece without putting pressure on vulnerable edges. If stacking plates, start with the largest and place a piece of kitchen paper between each one. Never stack cups upside down or one inside another, as both of these risk damage to the rim. Finally, do not store pieces in direct sunlight and be aware of sudden changes in temperature, which can cause glazes to crack.

Below: Take care of protruding parts, such as the pedestal base, neck rim and handles on this early 20th century handpainted Royal Worcester vase, when washing fragile porcelain.

REPAIRING A BROKEN PLATE

Ceramic plates that have clean breaks in one or two places can be repaired quite easily and quickly. Porcelain pieces are best repaired using epoxy resin, following the manufacturer's instructions, while white glue works best on pottery. In either case, make sure all of the pieces are clean and dry. Apply sparing amounts of the adhesive along the broken edge of one piece of porcelain or pottery, align the broken edge of the second piece of porcelain or pottery and gently coax the two pieces until they bond. This will squeeze out any excess adhesive, which is best removed while still wet; be careful to keep the pieces aligned as you do this. With the pieces joined, stretch several lengths of masking tape across the joint to keep them in place as the adhesive dries. With plates that are broken into more than two pieces, work on one at a time, ensuring that the first joint is totally dry before starting on the next.

1

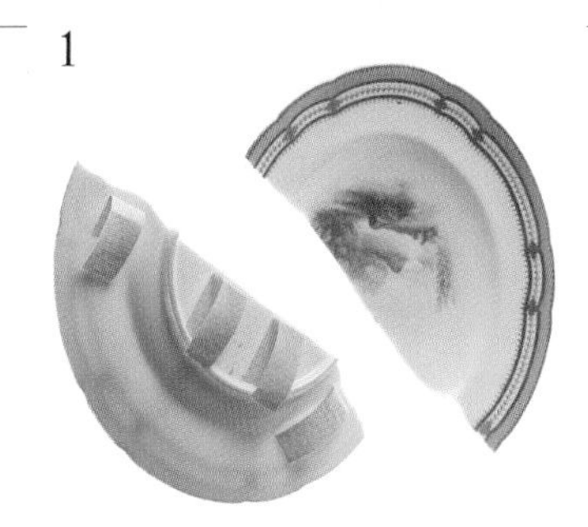

2

3

4

1. *Only attempt home repairs on clean breaks and, if your piece is valuable, always have it professionally repaired by a skilled craftsman.*

2. *Apply adhesive to one broken edge only. Use a suitable adhesive for the object that you are repairing, taking professional advice as necessary.*

3. *Use masking tape to secure the broken pieces together while the adhesive dries.*

4. *Stand the plate in a tray of sand to keep it upright and to prevent glue falling onto the drying surface.*

FOCUS ON: WEST GERMAN CERAMICS

From the 1950s to the 1970s, West German ceramics were dominated by mass-produced moulded pieces in a variety of shapes, and decorated by hand with modern or abstract colourful patterned glazes.

In West Germany, designers of ceramic wares in the immediate post-war period sought inspiration in abstract art and 1930s design, creating curving forms in primary colours and primarily linear or geometric or curving patterns. By the mid-1960s, designers were revelling in the freedom of the period to produce freely dripped and splashed glaze effects that were influenced by Pop Art and the moon landings. The result was a diverse range of vases – among them large, floor-standing examples in all manner of thick, often heavily textured and brightly coloured glazes, now referred to by the term "fat lava".

The popularity of such pieces was short-lived, however, and during the 1980s the style went out of fashion. Many pieces were thrown away or relegated to attics and charity shops. Yet despite the vehemence with which these pieces seem to have been hated, recent interest has sparked a reappraisal of fat lava ceramics, and a revival is underway. Already this is a hot market – prices are rising dramatically and are expected to rise further. The current desirability of such pieces has been increased through attempts by high street stores such as Habitat, Heal's, and Ikea to reproduce the look. Although these versions are unlikely to hold their value in the long term, they have done much to heighten awareness of the originals.

Highly accessible, fat lava pieces can be found at antiques fairs, and may turn up in charity shops at very low prices – under £30. Makers to look out for include Scheurich, Bay Keramik, Roth, and Ruscha. Among the notable designers are Gerda Heuckeroth, Hans Welling and Bodo Mans.

When looking for pieces, seek out the wildest and most outlandish shapes and glazes, which are likely to carry the highest values, but also the huge "floor vases", which can be worth over five times more than a standard-sized piece. Owing to recent health and safety regulations, many of the glaze colours and effects can never be repeated, making them even more desirable. Look for marks on the bases of pieces you find, which will help to identify them.

Bottom left: Large floor–standing pieces, such as this 1970s Bay Keramik jug vase, were prone to damage from vacuum cleaners and pets. The dripped vibrant yellow glaze is highly desirable.

Bottom right: The tapered, wasp–waisted form of this Dümler & Breiden vase is typical of the 1950s and early 1960s.

VINTAGE CLASSICS

This 1970s Roth Keramik no.312 vase is an iconic piece from the 1970s, and is one of the most striking pieces to emerge during this time. Nicknamed the "Guitar" vase by collectors, the dramatic, space–aged form is without precedent. The bold glossy orange is typical of the period, and the highly desirable 'lava' glaze highlights both the form and the pattern. Already being snapped up by design enthusiasts and collectors in the field, it can also be found with purple, yellow or blue glazes, which are rarer and more valuable.

Far left: *The single jug–like handle of this 1970s Scheurich no.401 vase is a recurring design motif found on many West German vases. Although brightly coloured, the flat glossy glaze is less interesting to some collectors.*

Centre: *The flame–like effect on this Scheurich 'Lora' series vase is made by layering glazes and then cutting back through them to reveal the underlying colours.*

Above: *The smooth coloured glaze contrasting against a black textured 'lava' glaze is a hallmark of Jopeko's production from the late 1960s–70s.*

BUYING GLASS

Right: *Not all cut glass is heavily cut in the Victorian style. Clyne Farquharson's pattern of stylised leaves on this 1930s Walsh Walsh vase is as modern today as it was when it was introduced.*

Below: *Whitefriars' iconic 1970s 'Drunken Bricklayer' vase, designed by Geoffrey Baxter in 1966, was once relegated to charity shops and flea markets. A style reappraisal has caused prices to rocket over the past decade.*

Glassware, including decanters, vases, glasses, plates, bowls, and bottles, exists in many forms – whether blown, moulded, or pressed – and colours. Like silver (see p.102), this is an ancient art form with a very rich history, and many fine pieces have survived the years.

Glassware that bears typical characteristics of a period style are more desirable than pieces that do not, so it is useful to be able to identify them. Several glassmaking milestones can help to establish the approximate date of a piece of glassware:

- The first was the development of lead crystal by George Ravenscroft in 1676, which allowed for the deep-cut surfaces that became fashionable during the late 18th and 19th centuries.
- The second was the advent of moulded glass, which allowed for the mass-production of glassware on a large scale. (Prior to this, it had been hand-blown and hand-moulded piece by piece.) Pieces that have visible seams have almost certainly been made using moulding techniques.
- A third milestone was the American invention in the 1820s of factory pressed glass, which led to the production of very cheap cut glass; pressed cut-glass pieces are noticeably lighter than original lead crystal pieces.

As well as using these milestones to date a piece, there are countless decorative characteristics that can help to make identification more precise. For example, by looking at the stems of 18th-century glasses and the shapes of their bowls, you can assess whether a piece is early or late Georgian; looking at the designs of cut glass can indicate whether a piece is Regency or Art Deco in style; while gilded beakers were a particular feature of late Neo-classical design.

A dominant feature of 20th-century glassmaking is the tendency toward producing art glass of exceptional quality, characterized by a wide range of innovative decorative finishes. Among the more exciting of these are Art Nouveau iridescent glass, the metallic sheen of which lent itself so perfectly to the fluid lines that were typical of the style; and pieces produced by the Murano glass factory in Venice in the 1950s and 1960s, involving the fusing together of murrines, or patches of glass, to vibrant effect.

When looking at glassware, check thoroughly for signs of damage

A CRITICAL EYE

Successful designs are often copied, particularly if demand outstrips supply and prices rise. Some copies are purely inspired by the originals, such as the vase shown here, but some are intended to deceive. Read books to learn about the colourways and shapes of originals, and visit dealers and auctions to handle authentic piece to build up a practical knowledge for the weight, colour tones and feel of originals. Marks, or the lack of them, can also help you distinguish copies from the real deal.

A 1990s Italian Dalla Valentina vase, in different colours and a different style than the original 'Pezzato' range designed in 1950 by Fulvio Bianconi for Venini.

and restoration – it is not unusual for stem glasses or vases to have their rims ground down to remove a chip (see p.101), for example. Tap the side of a glass or vase; a dull thud instead of a clear ringing sound might suggest a fault. Always look for makers' marks, but do not rely on these alone to establish authenticity, as they are often faked.

Left: *The graduated transparent yellow–green colour of this late Victorian Powell & Sons vase, created by adding uranium oxide to the glass mix, has led to collectors calling it 'Vaseline' glass.*

Below: *A Mid–century Modern classic, this Chance Bros. printed glass handkerchief vase, introduced in 1957, was inspired by a design by Fulvio Bianconi and Paolo Venini from c1949.*

FOCUS ON: DECANTERS

Below: Designed by Gio Ponti for Venini, this incalmo decanter resembles a stylised human figure. Vintage examples can cost less than new versions sold by the company today.

A hundred years ago, most middle-class households in Britain would have had a wine decanter. Originating in the early 18th century, the decanter grew in popularity along with the rise of the middle classes during the 19th century, and pieces were produced on a large scale – so much so that it became a staple of fine dining. However, the demand for such pieces waned during the first half of the twentieth century, particularly after World War II, when they went out of fashion, so dining became a more casual affair.

Objects of great beauty, these predominantly clear-glass vessels have been variously shaped over the decades and decorated with all manner of engraved, enamelled, or cut-glass designs. From early 18th-century tapering shapes, through Georgian urn or barrel shapes, to the complex patterned cut wares of the Victorian era, plenty of styles exist. In later years, under the influence of the Art Nouveau and Art Deco styles, colour was also a regular feature.

The decanter's fall from grace can, to some extent, be attributed to the fact that people have become more relaxed about serving wine from its original container. Also, in recent years there has been a degree of pomp attached to showing a bottle and its label in order to impress guests. And, with many wines being produced with the intention of their being drunk within three years, there is less need to decant wine as it is not so often laid down. Despite this, in these credit crunch times, with fewer people eating out, there is something to be said for the charm of these pieces and the elegance they can bring to entertaining at home.

When looking for pieces, you can usually identify the period in which a decanter was made. Many wine experts also claim a wine that is aerated by decanting is improved in taste. Prices will vary depending on what you find, but you can expect to find a 19th-century piece for £50 to £100. Avoid pieces with heavy staining, which may be difficult to clean, or with "crizzelling" (fine lines or cracks), which is terminal. If you are planning to use it for spirits, never buy a decanter without its original stopper as it will not be air-tight.

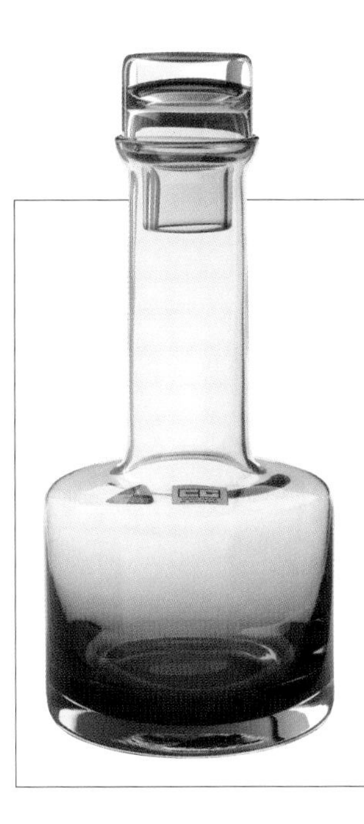

BETTER TO BUY OLD THAN NEW

20th century decanters are often over-looked, particularly if they look 'new'. This Caithness Glass 'Morven' decanter, designed in 1961 by Domhnall O'Broin, looks as modern today as it did nearly fifty years ago. Examples can currently be found for under £20, a fraction of the price of a new decanter from the high street. This, and examples by O'Broin's contemporaries Ronald Stennett-Willson and Frank Thrower, may prove to be wise investments as demand and prices look set to increase.

1. *The 'shaft and globe' form and this style of cutting are typically associated with the Victorian era.*

2. *This form, the mushroom stopper, and practical neck rings are associated with late Georgian decanters.*

3. *The tapering 'club' shaped body, flat inverted teardrop stopper, and cut design indicate this was made c1790.*

4. *The lack of sharpness of the edges indicate this 19th century Irish decanter is moulded rather than cut.*

CLEANING AND CARING FOR GLASS

The guidelines for cleaning and caring for glass are similar to those for ceramics (see p.92), and you can prolong the lifespan of your pieces if you care for them correctly. You are likely to have pieces on display as well as those for regular and occasional use, and they all benefit from being kept clean.

Glass on display will be kept either in a cabinet or on a shelf, and pieces exposed to the atmosphere in a room will obviously become dusty more quickly than those behind glass or wooden doors. For dusting glass, a soft cloth is the best option, handling each piece in turn. Watch the tap too! When it comes to washing glass, most pieces will shine having been washed in warm water with a little mild detergent. It pays to line the base of the sink with a tea towel to prevent breakages, and to wash one piece at a time. Use a toothbrush to clean dirt that has settled in cut-glass or engraved areas and a bottle brush for pieces with narrow necks, such as decanters. Rinse all glassware with warm water, and dry immediately using a clean linen tea towel to prevent drip marks. Jars, bottles, and decanters with narrow necks can be left to air-dry naturally with their stoppers or tops off.

REPAIRING A CHIPPED RIM

Unless a piece is extremely valuable – in which case you should seek professional help – it is possible to repair a chip to the rim of a glass by grinding the glass down using silicon-carbide paper. This paper is also known as "wet and dry", because it can be used with and without water. For very small chips, wrap dry paper around the handle of a wooden spoon and rub back and forth across the rim of the glass until the chip is no longer visible. For larger chips, you need to wear down the whole circumference of the glass if you want to avoid ending up with an uneven rim. The best way to do this is to lay a sheet of silicon-carbide paper on a work surface, and to grind the rim of the glass, gently, using a circular motion. Wetting the rim of the glass from time to time will prevent a build-up of glass dust.

Some glassware develops stubborn stains. This is particularly true of vases that are used regularly and develop watermarks and decanters used for storing port and red wine. Remove water marks from a vase by soaking it in a white vinegar and water solution for several days, then wash, rinse, and dry as described above. To clean a stained decanter, fill it with 15–20ml (3–4 teaspoons) of white vinegar and add 10ml (2 teaspoons) of salt. Shake for a minute or so, with the stopper in, and leave to stand overnight. Wash, rinse, and dry. And if nothing works, consult a professional.

Opposite, top: *As much a sculptural form as a functional vase, this pressed glass vase designed by Vladislav Urban in 1962 is typical of postwar Czech glass that is becoming increasingly desirable and valuable.*

Above: *Designed for Lemington Glass by Ronald Stennett-Willson in 1959, this set of 'Harlequin' tumblers provided a burst of colour when most British drinking wares were colourless.*

BUYING SILVER AND METALWARES

Right: Silver candlesticks can make great investments as well as being both practical and beautiful. This fine, early Georgian pair by the legendary silversmith Paul de Lamerie are at the top end of the market.

Below: Whilst this Neoclassical tea and coffee service by notable maker Paul Storr is made from solid silver, a similar, silver-plated set could be built up for a fraction of the cost of this fine late Georgian set.

Silverware – candlesticks, tea and coffee services, dinnerware, and cutlery – is widely available at antiques fairs and from specialist dealers. All silver has an intrinsic value as a metal as well as its value as a made item. Pieces go out of fashion or drop in value to below the value of the metal itself as a result and command high prices as a result of their maker, date and quality.

Most early pieces (pre-1750) were either cast from solid silver or raised from sheet silver. Typical pieces include candlesticks made from two or three solid components soldered together, or plates, bowls, and other simple forms with no obvious seams. From c1743 to 1840 many pieces were made from Old Sheffield plate, sheet silver fused to sheet copper, which was used to mass produce pieces in greater numbers – often copies of earlier forms. Look for pieces with obvious seams and with wear from use and polishing where the copper shows through. Electroplated pieces (often marked EPNS) emerged from the 1830s onward, with base metal forms being dipped into liquid silver solution and plated using an electric current; these tend to be brighter than Old Sheffield plate.

Examine the shape and decoration of the piece to make sure it is in keeping with the date suggested by the silver marks (see box). Note that the style of decoration (such as scrolling lines, gadrooning, complete absence of ornament) is as good an indication of date as the manner in which the decoration has been achieved (applied, embossed, or engraved).

Although most other metalwares are not marked as clearly as silver, many will have names or the maker's initials stamped on them. They can also be identified by style and decoration to some extent. Copper and pewter wares are particularly associated with the Arts and Crafts and Art Nouveau movements, while aluminium and stainless steel pieces are predominantly modern materials, used from the 1930s onward.

A CRITICAL EYE

Most British silver will have a number of marks that indicate the maker and quality of the silver, and when and where the piece was made. See pages 214-215 for more information. All these factors contribute to desirability and value – a notable maker, early date, unusual form, or a scarce assay office mark may make a piece sought–after. When you are looking at a pair of candlesticks, or a complete coffee service, make sure that all pieces bear the same marks.

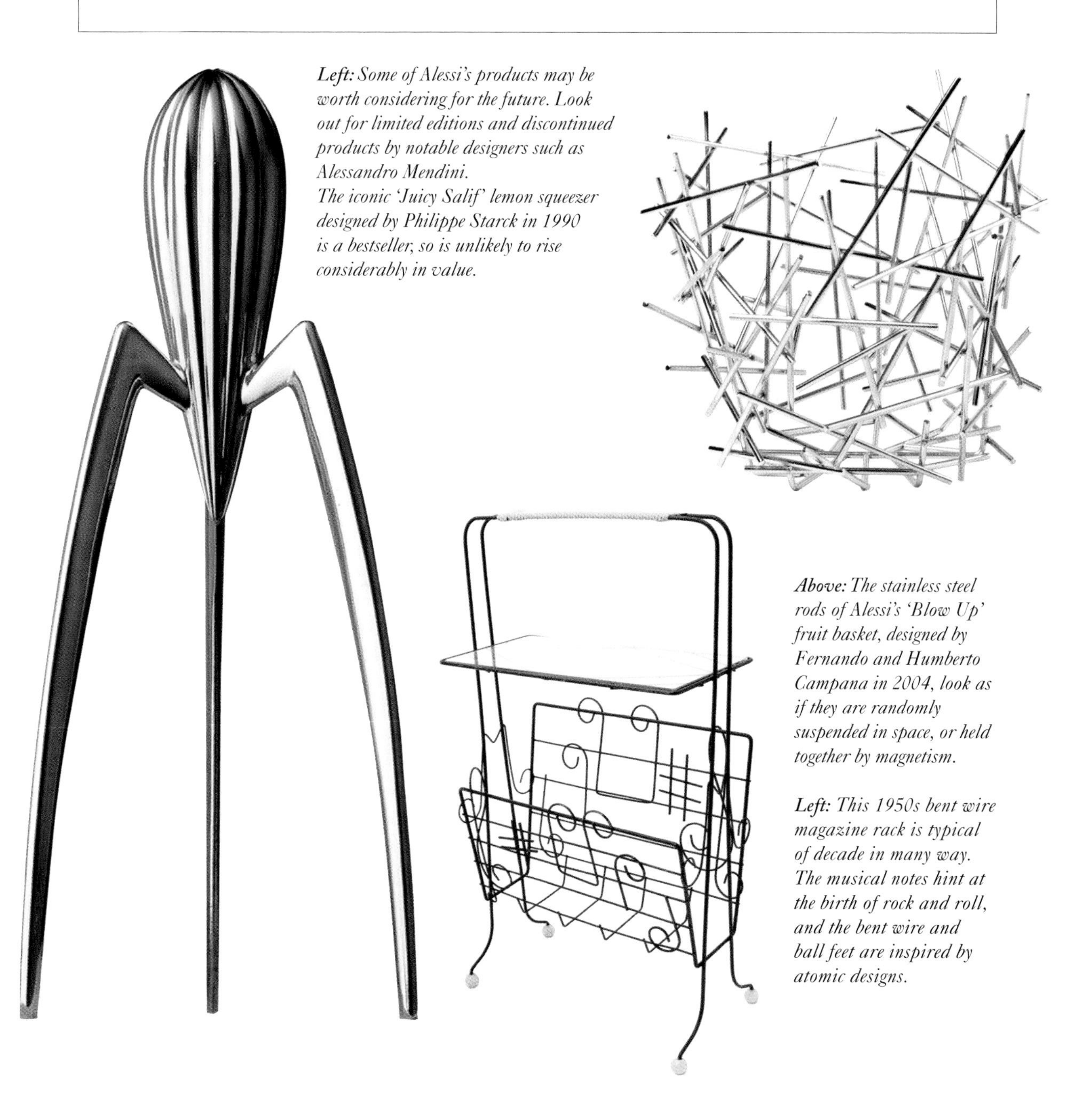

Left: *Some of Alessi's products may be worth considering for the future. Look out for limited editions and discontinued products by notable designers such as Alessandro Mendini. The iconic 'Juicy Salif' lemon squeezer designed by Philippe Starck in 1990 is a bestseller, so is unlikely to rise considerably in value.*

Above: *The stainless steel rods of Alessi's 'Blow Up' fruit basket, designed by Fernando and Humberto Campana in 2004, look as if they are randomly suspended in space, or held together by magnetism.*

Left: *This 1950s bent wire magazine rack is typical of decade in many way. The musical notes hint at the birth of rock and roll, and the bent wire and ball feet are inspired by atomic designs.*

FOCUS ON: POST-WAR METALWARE

Stainless steel homewares began to boom in the 1950s, their sleek forms epitomizing the "good design" tenets of modernism. Pieces could be produced at low cost, making them ideal candidates for mass production. Leading manufacturers included Viners, Old Hall, and Elkington, who began to produce a wide range of goods, from tea and coffee sets through toast racks, candlesticks, and cruet sets to beakers and goblets.

The interest in using stainless steel owed much to the avant-garde designs emerging in Scandinavia in the immediate post-war years. With the revolutionary Danish firm Georg Jensen leading the way, pieces designed by Arne Jacobsen and Henning Koppel, among others, demonstrated the stunning forms and finishes that could be achieved. In Britain, such designs began to influence a number of designer-craftsmen, several of whom studied at the Royal College of Art under Professor Robert Goodden. As well as adopting and adapting the fashionable Continental styles, these designers – David Mellor, Stuart Devlin, and Robert Welch among them – also struck out on their own. As well as producing a number of precious metal pieces under their own names, they also designed lines for Viners, Old Hall, and Elkington.

Until recently, their designs have been largely ignored by collectors and design historians. However, there has been a surge in interest and rising prices for the precious metalwares designed by Mellor, Devlin, and Welch, in particular those that display each designer's hallmark themes and motifs. Now is almost certainly the time to get on board and, if you cannot afford the unique precious metalwares, turn to the designers' "diffusion" lines produced in stainless steel. Look out for pieces that exemplify the style, such as a strong Scandinavian aesthetic in terms of clean-lined forms, functional pieces, and surfaces free of embellishment. Robert Welch pieces include Old Hall tea sets, which he designed when employed by the firm as their consultant (from 1955). Devlin's "hallmark" style is shiny silver contrasted with bark-textured gold, a look that was influential and unique to Britain. Good examples of stainless steel pieces can be found for under £150, with many costing

Below: The tapered flutes of Robert Welch's classic stainless steel 'Campden' triple candleholder, designed in 1957 for Old Hall.

VINTAGE CLASSICS

In 1972, Viners commissioned Stuart Devlin to design a range of stainless steel wares in his characteristic style for mass production. The "Devlin Collection" comprised around nine shapes including goblets, beakers, and bowls – all with the shiny stainless steel juxtaposed against textured gold-plated areas. Examples currently cost from £5-30, with original boxes making a piece more desirable. Adding a unique sparkle to a table setting, now could be a good time to buy, as these are sure to become sought-after classics of their day.

Right: *Even the humble toast rack can be of interest – Robert Welch's 'Campden' toastrack, designed in 1957, won a prestigious Design Centre award.*

under £40, while canteens of cutlery can be cheaper than modern ones. Because stainless steel is a non-tarnishing metal, most pieces are in very good condition. They look great in a table setting and they capture the current interest in Mid-century Modern design perfectly.

Below: *Perhaps Robert Welch's most important design for Old Hall, the stylish 'Alveston' teaset of 1964 included the first metal teapot to have a spout integral with the body. The forms are strongly reminiscent of many Scandinavian designs.*

CLEANING AND CARING FOR METAL

The antique metals in your home may range from silverware, pewter, and brass to aluminium, stainless steel, and chrome. As with glass and ceramics, many of these pieces may be on display, while others will have regular or occasional use for serving food and drink.

Most metals develop a patina as they age, just as leather and wood do (see pp.68 and 70), and when cleaning them it is important not to do so too vigorously or it could remove the patina, thus reducing the potential value of an item. All metals can be dusted, using a soft clean cloth or brush. Polished metals, such as silver, brass, and copper, and non-corrosive metals such as aluminium, stainless steel, and chrome, can be washed in warm soapy water, using a mild detergent. They should be rinsed and dried immediately to avoid water marks. It is best to avoid washing bronze and pewter, as their patina is particularly significant. You can still dust them, however, and should do so frequently. When it comes to polishing metals, always use a proprietary cleaner, making sure you follow the manufacturer's instructions.

Above: This set of four early 20th century silver goblets are badly tarnished. Although they would benefit from a good clean, be aware that every time silver or silver-plated items are cleaned a minute layer of silver is removed from the surface.

Take particular care when cleaning and polishing metalware with special finishes, such as engraving and chasing, which involve cutting or pressing into the surface of the metal – you risk wearing away the engraved areas and making chasing less crisp. Cloisonné and champlevé finishes also need special attention. Any pieces that display broken edges, weak soldering joints, loose enamels, or similar damage are best worked on by a professional. Avoid heavily scrubbing or scouring a metal piece and the temptation to put it in a dishwasher.

You can prolong the life of your metalware by taking greater care of it. Dust pieces as part of your regular household routine, and clean or polish them sparingly. Always use clean cloths for polishing, and do not be tempted to use polish for one metal on another. Wash metalware that has been used for serving food and drink immediately to prevent excessive tarnishing. Store pieces wrapped in acid-free paper or in clean linen or cotton sheeting.

REMOVING DENTS FROM METAL

It is possible to restore the shape of a dented piece of metalware, especially if the piece has a relatively simple form. In most cases, soft metals like pewter can be can worked successfully by hand. Whether a square form has become slightly twisted or a round form a little distorted, simply work the piece gently and slowly, applying even pressure all around, in order to bring it back to its original shape. Assess the soundness of the metal before starting, however, to make certain that it will not split or crease if you work it too hard. For dents in hard metals, like copper, to prevent additional dents from forming you need to support the inside of the piece as you work on the surface – best done by shaping a piece of wood to fit inside the copper item. This can be time-consuming, however, and you may prefer to seek the help of a professional.

***Left:** The coppery patches on the stand of this Old Sheffield Plate teapot are a result of frequent, ardent cleaning and wear, which has removed the silver plated surface, revealing the copper base beneath.*

***Right:** The hammered surface effect on this Art Nouveau copper jardinière by John Pearson sparkles when polished. Arts and Crafts and Art Nouveau copper is becoming increasingly sought–after.*

BUYING LIGHTING

Below: The 'Triennale' standard lamp was designed in the 1950s by award-winning designer Gino Sarfatti for Italian company Arteluce. The primary colours of the shades are repeated in the handles that angle the lights.

Lights are relative newcomers to the world of antiques, with the earliest examples dating back just one hundred years, following the excitement of the widespread use of electricity in the domestic environment. Despite this, the choice of light fitting is wide and varied, with some truly innovative designs to look out for.

Each style period from the last century has yielded lamp and light designs that characterize the period. Typical features to look out for include Arts and Crafts table lamps with hand-hammered copper bases, and the exquisite Art Nouveau leaded glass lampshades produced by Louis Comfort Tiffany at the turn of the 20th century. The advance of technology in the 1920s and 1930s brought geometric, industrial-looking Bauhaus lamps with Bakelite or opal glass shades and elegant, streamlined Art Deco designs using chromed steel and glass.

The soft sculptural forms of the mid-20th century were followed by the bright plastics of the Pop age, the neon strips of Postmodernism, and the pared-back, minimalist forms of the High Tech age. In recent years, industrial lights have become popular – look for sandblasted and polished lights from film studios, machinists' lights with articulated stems, ships' lights, and even runway lamps.

The chandelier has also made a comeback. Examples can be found from all periods, including antique candle or gas chandeliers that have been modified for the electric equivalent, and 20th-century versions in which the candles have been replaced by all manner of cut-glass drops, painted metal flowers, glass cylinders, or coloured discs.

Shades can be found in a wide range of materials, shapes, and sizes. They include pretty French ridged-glass bells, enamelled shades from factories, and white opaline domes and balls, and can usually be fitted to existing ceiling-mounted fittings, avoiding the extra cost of replacing wiring by a professional electrician.

As with all antiques, check pieces closely for signs of wear and tear or obvious restoration. Check that shades claiming to be original are just that and that all components from any one light belong to the same era. Look for chips and cracks on glass pieces, tears in fabric or paper, and dents to metal shades and bases. Almost all vintage fittings should have a maker's label, which will help you to date a piece with greater accuracy.

VINTAGE CLASSICS

Danish designer Poul Henningsen stated that the aim of lighting "is to beautify the home and those who live there; to make the evening restful and relaxing." Originally designed for the Langelinie Pavilion restaurant in Copenhagen, his 'Artichoke' fulfills that aim. The overlapping copper leaves hide the brightness of the bulb, giving a warm, diffused light. Unsurprisingly, it has since become a classic lighting design.

A Danish Louis Poulsen 'PH Artichoke' pendant lampshade, designed by Poul Henningsen in 1958.

1. *Verner Panton's designs are recalled in this 1970s Swedish Fagerluchts plastic lamp, with it's hemispherical rise–and–fall shade.*

2. *The crackle effects of Shattaline's brightly coloured resin lampbases, designed c1965 by Lewen Tugwell, are unique to each piece. The shade is an original.*

3. *This extravagant 1970s chandelier, comprised of clear and amber glass flowers, was probably made on Murano.*

4. *This Lalique yellow 'Soleil' plafonnier, made from 1926-47, typifies Art Deco style.*

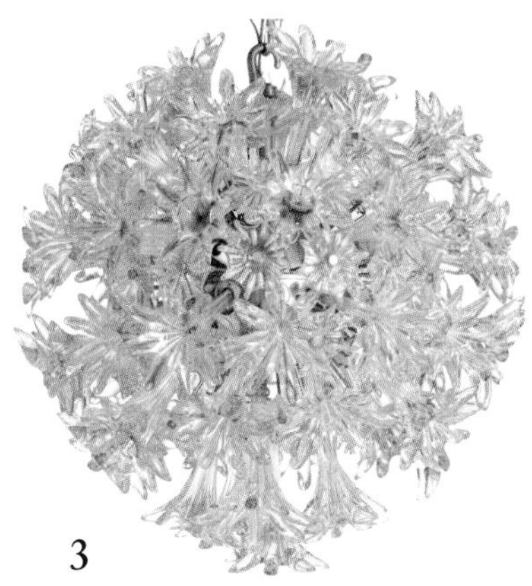

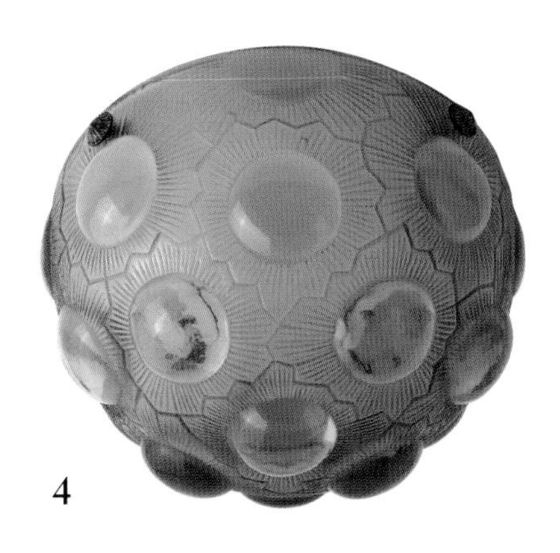

BUYING TEXTILES

Above: Home-made during the 1950s, this embroidered cushion shows popular themes in period design. These include the birth of rock and roll, fashionable dances, the growth of television, and romantic foreign climes such as Hawaii.

Made for many centuries, textiles have a relatively short lifespan in antique terms as they are prone to wear, damage and deterioration. Among the earliest surviving textiles are tapestries from late 17th-century France. Verdure tapestries – natural woodland scenes, flat-woven in a limited range of greens, blues, and browns – in particular command very high prices. You might find less costly mid- to late 19th-century reproductions.

Samplers were created from the 16th to the 19th centuries by individuals demonstrating their needlework skills. Early samplers were tall and thin, while from the 18th century they tended to be square. Initially showing embroidery stitches and motifs in an almost random fashion, they later become more structured. In samplers from the mid-18th century onward, as well as motifs and the needleworker's name you may find additional elements such as the letters of the alphabet, numerals, pictorial images, and verses.

Prior to the invention of the steam-powered loom in the 1780s, woven fabrics were primarily exquisite silk works intended for a wealthy clientele. Examples in the Rococo or early Neo-classical styles (see Know Your Style, pp. 140) can be found today but are rare and expensive. After this time, with manufacturing time having improved, many textiles can be found in complex repeating patterns in a range of colours, including florals, paisleys, and stripes.

Early European printed fabrics were inspired by 17th-century Indian imports. The biggest name in the field was the Oberkampf works at Jouy-en-Josas, in France. Using copperplate printing methods, the company produced from the late 18th century the monochrome prints in reds and blues on white cotton, showing allegorical rural scenes, but also with Classical, chinoiserie and floral patterns. Vintage examples of these toiles de Jouy are sought after and examples made well into the 19th century can still be found.

From the end of the 19th century and well into the 20th century, fabrics clearly represent the trends of their times. Look out for William Morris's traditionally hand-woven Arts and Crafts textiles and C.F.A. Voysey's Art Nouveau repeating patterns, both of which depict nature using stylized motifs. During the Art Deco era, an obsession with the industrial age was manifested in geometric patterns, but there were also abstract designs inspired by the Cubist art movement. Mid-century designs focus on stylized natural motifs or abstract, atomic or scientific designs, or are in-keeping with the prevailing post-war focus on domesticity, while classics from the 1960s and 1970s tend toward psychedelia and Pop Art.

A CRITICAL EYE

An ongoing European interest in the East reached a new peak in the Victorian era, with rugs being imported from Persia, Turkey, and China. While you need expert advice on identifying a rug's specific origins, there are ways of telling whether a rug has been machine- or handmade. Traditionally made by knotting the weft (horizontal) threads around the warp (vertical) threads, the knots are clearly visible on the underside of a handmade rug and absent on a machine-made one. The fringe on a handmade rug is made from the uncut warp strands, while machine-made rugs have easily spotted applied fringes.

Introduced in 1883 by England's Zeigler & Co, Zeigler rugs were made in Iran for the Western market and are typified by a soft muted palette and an all-over pattern.

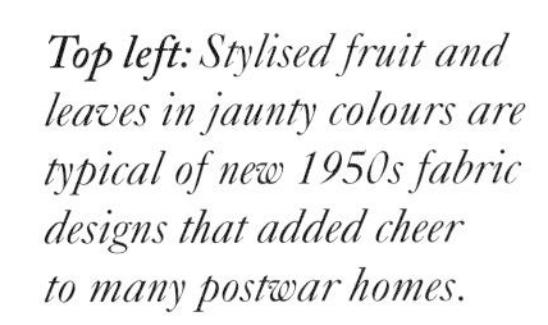

Top left: *Stylised fruit and leaves in jaunty colours are typical of new 1950s fabric designs that added cheer to many postwar homes.*

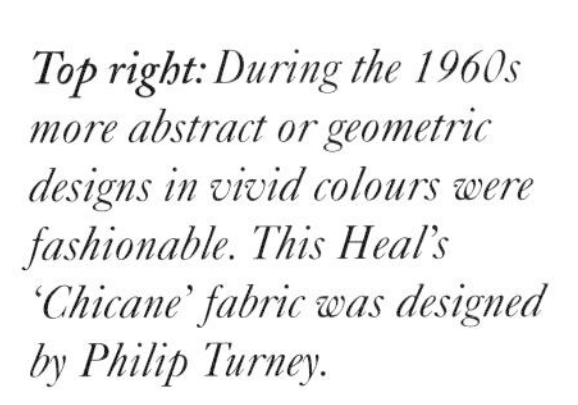

Top right: *During the 1960s more abstract or geometric designs in vivid colours were fashionable. This Heal's 'Chicane' fabric was designed by Philip Turney.*

Bottom left: *One of William Morris' most complex, expensive and successful designs, 'Strawberry Thief was introduced in 1883.*

Bottom right: *18th century French toile de Jouy or toile de Nantes, such as this Petit-pierre Frères 'Panurge dans L'île des Lanternes' is both scarce and valuable, particularly in large sizes.*

Above: *Designed by Lucienne Day, Britain's leading postwar textile designer, 'Calyx' defined the look of postwar textile design. Named after the leaf–like structure that protects a flowerbud, it was first seen at the Festival of Britain in 1951.*

CLEANING AND CARING FOR TEXTILES

Vintage and antique textiles in your home may range from samplers and tapestries through quilts to rugs and carpets. Some may be very delicate, while others are more robust. You can prolong the life of your textiles by using and storing them appropriately. All textiles should be stored or displayed away from heat sources, such as fires and radiators, and out of direct sunlight to avoid bleaching of the colours. Valuable rugs and carpets should be protected from the pressure of heavy furniture so that isolated areas do not become worn.

All vintage and antique textiles need cleaning from time to time. At the very least, this means dusting them. Most items can be dusted using a vacuum cleaner on a low setting. Carpets and rugs will benefit from a beating before being vacuumed, which can be done outside, with the rug attached to a clothesline. This will help to force out the loose dust, but also to dislodge more stubborn dirt particles. Always beat the back of the rug, not the front. When vacuuming, it is important to follow the direction of the pile, if the rug has one. The more delicate the rug, the lower the vacuum setting should be.

When it comes to cleaning, any textile of reasonable value should be cleaned professionally. This is particularly the case for those that are not colourfast. For pieces of lesser value, you could undertake the cleaning yourself (see box). As with the upholstery in your home, there are numerous ways in which to deal with obvious, identifiable stains, and a good book on household cleaning will list them.

Textiles are best rolled for storing, as folding them could leave permanent creases in the fabric. The best method is to roll them around cardboard tubes, with a layer of acid-free tissue paper. Never wrap textiles in plastic to store them, as it tends to sweat and can cause mould to develop. Textiles stored in cupboards, blanket boxes, or chests of drawers should be protected against moths.

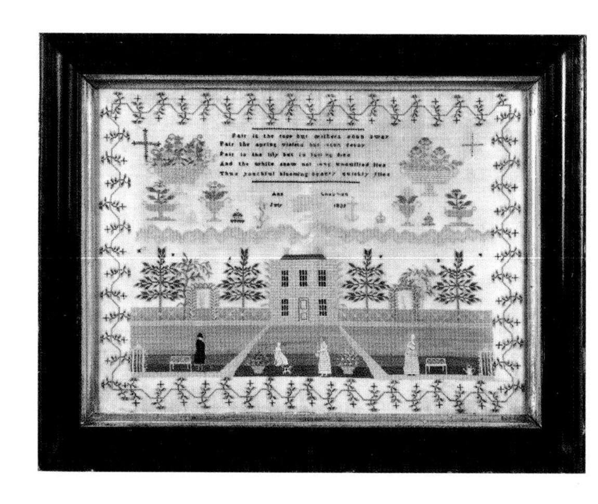

Right: *The type and decorative nature of motifs shown, together with the condition, affect the desirability of samplers. Often made by young girls, this fine example was embroidered by Ann Chapman in 1839.*

CLEANING NON COLOUR-FAST ITEMS

Cover your item with nylon monofilament screening and remove dust through the screening using a vacuum cleaner. Lay the item on the screening and cover thickly with hand-hot potato starch. Leave for ten minutes then brush off. Repeat as necessary.

CLEANING SMALL COLOUR-FAST ITEMS

Remove dust (as above). place item on nylon monofilament screening and place in a tray of cold water. Drain and replace with hot (but not scalding) water and mild wool detergent. Dab with a sponge and repeat using fresh soapy water until no more dirt can be removed. Rinse by dabbing the item with clean soap-free water. Pin the item to a board or table to regain its shape and either dab gently with clean towelling or blotting paper or, alternatively, use the low-heat setting of a hairdryer.

WASHING AND DRYING

For textiles that you can wash yourself, it helps to have a container in which you can lay the piece flat – if at all possible, you want to avoid folding or scrunching vintage textiles while washing them. Start by pre-soaking the textile in cold water. Gently push it beneath the surface, helping it to become saturated, and leave for five to ten minutes. Drain the water, and refill, this time with warm soapy water (use a mild detergent, suitable for hand-washing delicate fabrics). Work the soapy water into the textile to remove the dirt. Replace the soapy water with several changes of clean warm water for rinsing. Drain off as much water as possible without wringing the textile, and remove any excess by patting with a clean, preferably white, towel. Remove from the container and allow to dry naturally on a flat surface.

SOFT FURNISHINGS

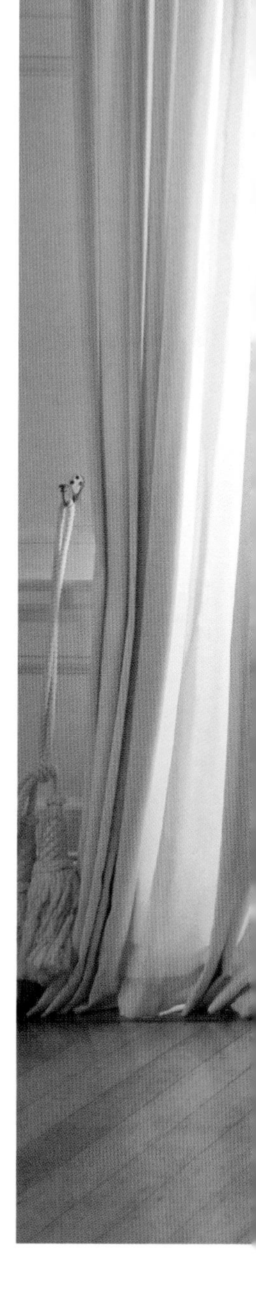

Like the all-important icing on a cake, every successful interior only comes alive when topped off by soft furnishings. Finishing touches such as curtains, pillows, throws and rugs should never be the last things you consider, as they have extraordinary transformative powers and can make or break a scheme. Not only do they soften any harsh architectural lines, they provide accents of colour, can introduce pattern, build on mood, and enhance overall comfort.

Window treatments make the strongest impact on a room. Curtains are more expansive, blinds less intrusive, but both frame a window and soften its geometrical lines as well as providing privacy and keeping in the warmth. With so many fabrics to choose from you can get just the look you want. Bear in mind that pattern is uplifting and eyecatching; plains are bold or recessive, depending on colour; linen is understated; velvet and silk are luxurious; and cotton is superbly versatile and drapes well. Generous curtains look much nicer than skimpy ones so allow enough material to skim or puddle on the floor and gather in plump fashion at the top. If windows are tall a pelmet will bring a sense of grandeur, but used in a low ceilinged room will foreshorten walls so avoid. When choosing patterned fabric, large-scale motifs will look better on big windows in big spaces, while small-scale motifs suit smaller windows and rooms. For a light feel to predominate pick a pattern with a pale, neutral ground. To create flowing effects put up tie-backs or hold-backs so that the fabric can drape beautifully, and to increase privacy use voiles.

Below: Piling your bed high with an assortment of cushions creates the perfect space for relaxing and dreaming of your next purchases.

Once window treatments have been settled upon, build on the effect with cushions, throws and rugs. If you have a collection on display you may want to pick out one or two shades within it to use as accent colours in soft furnishings – one or two

Above: A gold painted rococo-style sofa is placed in front of large windows, dressed with opulent and translucent curtains that gently pool on the floor, creating a feeling of luxury and elegance.

cushions is enough to make the connection. Throws can be used to give new life to old sofas and chairs, but can also look inviting in their own right draped and layered over furniture. A rug will bring warmth underfoot and gives you another chance to introduce colour, pattern and texture.

REVIVING ANTIQUES

RENOVATION

Below: The 18th- century walnut chest-on-stand shown here had been stored in a dirty attic for many years, so required the use of a very strong cleaning solution. Pre-mixed commercial cleaning and reviving mixtures are available if you are reluctant to mix your own. N.B. you should always be extremely careful when mixing and using chemicals. Follow the advice on commercial products and wear safety goggles and gloves where appropriate. It is essential that all such mixtures are stored well away from children and pets.

Dust, dirt and sticky grime allowed to accumulate on furniture gradually dulls the surface patina and in extreme cases, masks the figuring and grain of the wood. Use the cleaning techniques and solutions described here to remove these undesirable residues and, as long as the underlying surface finish is sound, revive the surface patina of your pieces

You will need two strengths of cleaning and reviving mixture, either the strong Solution A or the weaker Solution B. Which you need to use will depend on how dirty the surface is; Solution A should only be needed if the piece has been neglected for a long time. N.B. Pre-mixed commercial cleaning and reviving mixtures are available if you are reluctant to mix your own.

Solution A: In a 500ml glass jar, mix 4 parts white vinegar; 4 parts boiled linseed oil; 4 parts white spirit; 1 part methylated spirits; and 3–4 drops household ammonia. Make about 250ml of the mixture.

Solution B: In a 500ml glass jar, mix 4 parts white spirit with 1 part boiled linseed oil; again make about 250ml.

Start the cleaning process by removing all surface dust from your piece so you can see properly the extent of the underlying dirt. Use a soft-bristled dusting brush, working the bristles into any detailing to tease out all the dust. If the piece looks simply dull and dirty, follow step 2 (Clean and Revive) opposite. If it is badly neglected and thickly grimy, then mix a quantity of solution A as above and follow step 1 opposite (Remove Sticky Dirt and Grime). Performing a thorough clean-and-revive as shown opposite is a good idea every year or two depending on where your piece is housed, but to avoid needing to do so more often, dust the piece regularly, and re-wax or re-oil every month or two.

MATERIALS

Soft bristled dusting brush | Two glass jars, each with a capacity of at least 500ml (for cleaning-reviving solutions A and B) | White vinegar | Boiled linseed oil | White spirit| Methylated spirits | Household ammonia | Coarse, lint-free cotton rags | Wire wool, Grade 000 | Metal cleaners and polishes for any metal hardware on the furniture (such as brass, copper, iron and steel) | Cotton wool | Cotton buds | Masking tape | Scissors | Soft, lint-free rags | Boiled linseed oil, beeswax polish (tinted or clear) or one of the types of French polish (which of these will depend on the type of finish to be repaired)

1. REMOVE STICKY DIRT AND GRIME

Dampen a pad of coarse, lint-free cotton rag with cleaning solution A and, using a circular motion, rub the pad vigorously over the entire piece. The solution should start to dissolve the dirt, soiling the pad, so turn it and recharge with solution as necessary, and replace the pad when it is too dirty. In extreme cases where the cotton pad does not remove the dirt, dip a ball of grade-000 wire wool into the solution, squeeze out any excess and rub it lightly over the surface in the direction of the grain. Keep wiping the dissolved dirt off the surface with a cloth and replace the wire wool when necessary.

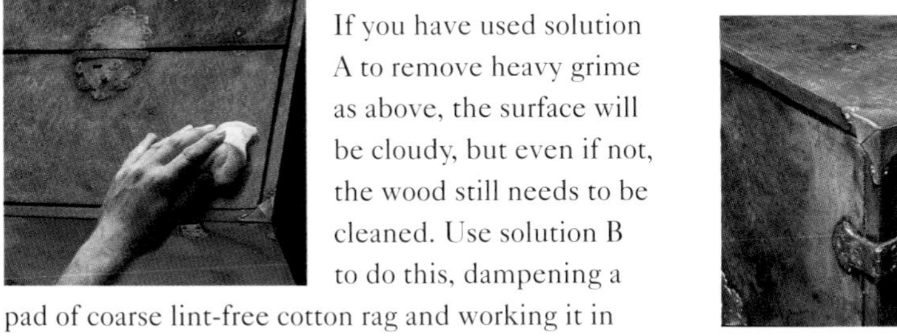

2. CLEAN AND REVIVE

If you have used solution A to remove heavy grime as above, the surface will be cloudy, but even if not, the wood still needs to be cleaned. Use solution B to do this, dampening a pad of coarse lint-free cotton rag and working it in vigorous circular motions as described above, again turning and recharging the pad as necessary. When you have finished, wipe the surface with a new cotton pad dampened with white spirit.

3. CLEAN METAL FITTINGS

Now is the time to clean any metal fittings there might be, such as hinges, locks, finger plates, pulls and corner brackets . Choose a proprietary cleaner to suit the metal or alloy from which the fitting is made; brass, copper and iron are the most common ones. Follow the manufacturer's instructions to the letter, and take care not to overclean since this can remove desireable patination. Apply cleaning solutions very carefully using a cotton bud or cotton wool, taking particular care not to get any solution on the surrounding wood. You can be sure that the wood will be properly protected by applying masking tape, cut to shape, to surrounding areas.

4. OIL, WAX OR POLISH

To protect and revive the surface further, apply a new coat of the original finish with a soft, lint-free rag, buffing to a shine with another soft, lint-free rag. The finish on antique furniture will be made up from either oil, wax or French polish (which may be overlaid with wax). Consult an antique dealer if you are uncertain about the finish and how to care for it.

REPAIRING A SCRATCH

Some damage to the surface of antique furniture resulting from accidents or general wear and tear is to be expected, and small dents and holes, along with fine and deep scratches, are common. While there are techniques for disguising them, it is worth remembering that rare and valuable pieces that are damaged may be considered more authentic than a repaired equivalent. It is always wise to consult an antique exert about what you should (or shouldn't) do to a valuable piece, particularly if you are planning to sell it. The value of a more commonplace piece is likely to be affected less.

Groups of small holes in wood are the result of insect infestation, mainly woodworm. If extensive, seek professional advice, but treat superficial damage with a commercial woodworm-killing fluid, and repair as described below.

Fine cracks result from the expansion and contraction of the wood due to changes in humidity. Along with small holes, these cracks can be treated with wax crayons designed for retouching furniture. Heat a piece of the appropriate colour with a naked flame, then cool slightly and press into the hole or crack with a knife. Once set, rub with the back of a piece of sandpaper to smooth the surface. Repolish the area.

Small dents and minor bruises in solid wood, but not veneered surfaces, can be raised using moisture and heat. Wipe the damaged area with white spirit to remove any wax. Dampen three lint-free rags with water and centre them, one on top of the other, on the bruise. Press an iron, on its lowest setting, on the rags for up to 30 seconds to swell the wood. Repeat, allowing it to cool, between applications.

For scratches to French polished surfaces, follow the steps shown opposite.

MATERIALS

Magnifying glass | French polish | Cotton buds | White spirit | Methylated spirits | Teaspoon | Small, shallow container (such as an old saucer) | Small, fine-tipped artist's brush | Scalpel | Liquid metal polish | Soft, lint-free cotton rag | Tinted beeswax furniture polish

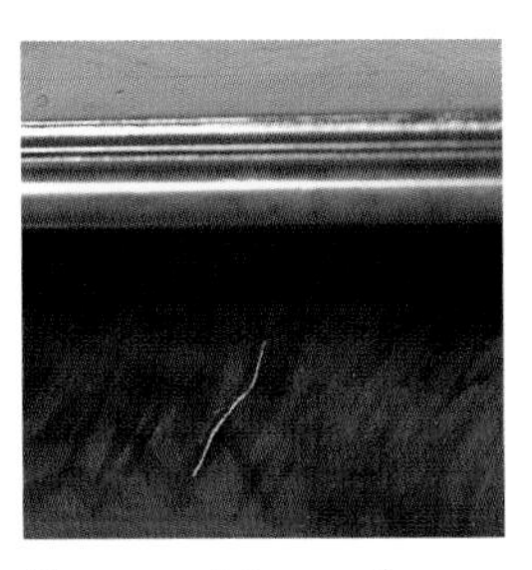

1. ASSESS THE DAMAGE Fine scratches in oiled or waxed surfaces can be disguised with a little shoe polish of the right colour rubbed on with a lint-free cloth, then buffed with a soft cloth. Commercial scratch removers are also an option and work by dissolving the layers of wax a little and re-forming them smoothly. Follow the manufacturer's application instructions. For deeper scratches on French polished surfaces such as this, start by identifying the exact colour of the wood surrounding the damaged area. Closely examine the piece, using a magnifying glass if necessary, then choose the shade of brown that is closest to the colour you wish to match.

2. CLEAN THE SURFACE Before you apply the French polish it is essential that the area is completely clean, or else the new polish will not adhere properly to the surface. Dissolve and remove any old layers of surface wax, using white spirit on a cotton bud. Rub the moistened bud very carefully back and forth over the scratch.

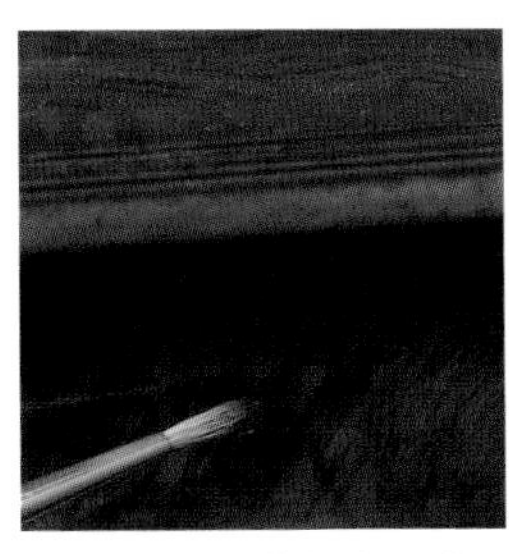

3. APPLY THE POLISH Some time before you are ready to start, place a teaspoonful of the French polish in a shallow container. Exposure to the air for 10–30 minutes will somewhat stiffen its consistency. Dip in a fine-tipped artist's brush and apply a thin layer to the scratch. The polish will harden, sinking into the scratch as it does so. Allow this first layer to harden for 4 hours, then apply a second layer in the same way. Allow this to harden, too, then build up additional layers. The final layer should set slightly raised from, and just overlapping, the surrounding area. Cover the polish in the container to preserve its consistency between applications.

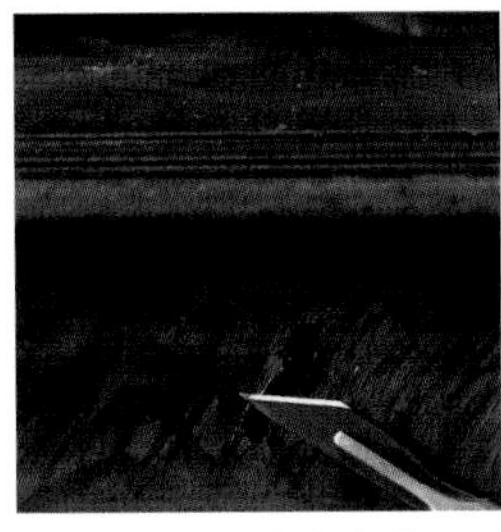

4. CUT THE POLISH FLUSH
Leave the polish to dry for a further 12 hours after which time it will have hardened completely. Take a scalpel blade and place the side of it very carefully at slightly less than 90° to one end of the repaired scratch. Very gently, taking great care not to allow the blade to slip and cut into the surrounding finish or wood (or your fingers!), push the blade across the surface in order to cut the polish flush with the surrounding area.

5. REPOLISH THE SURFACE
Moisten a cotton bud with liquid metal polish and lightly rub it back and forth along the length of the new surface to burnish it. Next, help to blend the repair into the area around it: with a soft, lint-free cloth, spread a thin layer of beeswax polish over the whole side of the piece on which the repair has been done. Finally, use a clean, soft cloth to buff the whole area to a shine.

OAK GRAIN EFFECT

Throughout history wood has been used in all manner of ways, from buildings and boats to furniture and tools. Due to its hard-wearing qualities and its ability to be transformed from a tree trunk into decorative items, wood has been used throughout the majority of homes over the years.

Wood can be categorized into two kinds: hardwoods and softwoods. Many softwood varieties come from fast-growing trees and are therefore available in large amounts. Varieties include fir, spruce, pine and cedar. These trees tend to produce a close grain with few markings, and are not regarded as being as attractive as their hardwood counterparts. Hardwoods, such as walnut, oak, mahogany and maple, have intricate grain patterns, making them more desirable, but they grow slower than softwoods, making them more scarce. During the 17th century, fashionable home-owners used expensive solid hardwoods in the manufacture of their furniture and decorations. This consequently produced a shortage of hardwoods as demand outgrew supply. Wood veneers were introduced to help reduce the amount of quality wood used to build furniture. Cheaper softwoods were used to construct an item and then covered in a thin sheet of hardwood. However, veneers did not solve the basic problem and the demand for hardwoods remained high. Another solution was needed and the practise of wood graining was born.

The technique of painting cheaper softwood to look like expensive hardwood has been popular since the 17th century. You could, for example, transform dull cupboard doors with an oak grain effect by following these steps.

MATERIALS
Paints and glazes using the artist's oils and materials shown right | Wood primer/undercoat | 5cm (2in) standard decorator's paintbrush | Clean cotton rags | White spirit | Small badger softener brush | 1cm (½in) flat flitch brush | Matter varnish |

1. PREPARE THE WOOD Before you start to paint an oak grain effect, the wooden doors must be prepared by priming or undercoating each one. Once this has been done, apply two coats of paint 5 (see paint and glaze specifications opposite) and leave it to dry overnight. Once dry, paint glaze 4 roughly over the centre panel and the frame.

2. CREATE THE GRAIN
Concentrate on the middle panel, and using a 5cm (2in) decorator's brush, drag the bristles from the top downwards, through the glaze. Move your brush in parallel lines that overlap slightly, in order to establish a grain effect. Once the middle panel is done, work along the top and the bottom of the frame in horizontal sweeps. Lastly direct the brush vertically along the left and right sides of the frame. After each sweep, clean the bristles with white spirit to remove any excess glaze.

3. ADD TEXTURE
Using a small badger softener, tap (flog) the sides of the bristles on the glaze in overlapping lines, working in the direction of the grain to create the pores of oak grain. Dry for 24 hours. Use a clean cotton rag to apply a thin coat of transparent oil glaze over the centre panel. After 15 minutes apply glaze 3 using a 1cm (½in) flat fitch. Begin just off centre and work outwards (see picture). Practise first on off-cuts of wood.

4. FLICK THE GLAZE
Continue creating the oak grain pattern so that it fills around a third of the centre panel. When you are happy with the pattern, using a large badger softener brush, gently flick the bristles over the wet glaze. This technique should be worked from the outside edge of the panel inwards. Always work towards the middle of the grain. It is a good idea to perfect your technique on a rough piece of wood first.

5. FINISH THE GRAIN EFFECT
Repeat the previous two steps to finish the heart graining on the centre of the door. Then, using a small badger softener brush, lightly flog the panel using the same technique as before.

6. APPLY THE GLAZE
Paint glaze 2 over the whole frame, then drag a small badger softener through the glaze at an angle to highlight the dark and light grain colours. Begin at the top and bottom edges of the frame then the sides, working in the direction of the grain. Flog the sides and leave to dry for 24 hours. Coat the wood with matter varnish.

The box below contains 'recipes' that should be used to make up the paints and glazes mentioned in the steps.

PAINTS AND GLAZES

1 Artist's oils: 3 parts burnt umber, 1 part black. Medium: 3 parts transparent oil glaze, 2 parts white spirit. Ratios in glaze: 1 part pigments,40 parts medium.

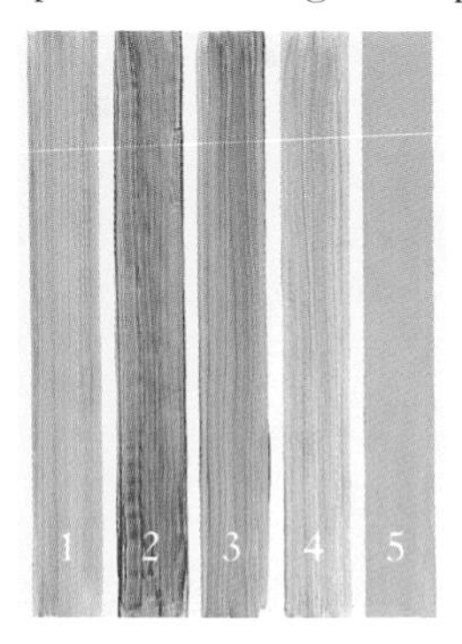

2 Artist's oils: 2 parts raw sienna, 1 part raw umber. Medium: 3 parts transparent oil glaze, 2 parts white spirit. Ratios in glaze: 1 part pigments, 7 parts medium.

3 Artist's oils: 2 parts raw sienna, 1 part raw umber. Medium: 4 parts transparent oil glaze, 5 parts white spirit. Ratios in glaze: 1 part pigment, 8 parts medium.

4 Artist's oils; 7 parts raw sienna, 3 parts raw umber. Medium: 3 parts transparent oil glaze, 2 parts white spirit. Ratios in glaze: 1 part pigments, 12 parts medium.

5 Bamboo coloured eggshell paint.

CREATING AGED PAINT

An aged piece of furniture that has been well-loved and used over the years possesses a special charm all of its own. The scratches, dents, flaking paint and accumulation of dirt all contribute to its appeal. Any piece of furniture or paint decoration will invariably show signs of age as the years go by, but if you have a new item that you want to transform using antique effects, there are many you can try. There are paints, glazes and various techniques, including crackle and antiquing glazes, spattering, dusting and distressing that you could try to produce the popular 'shabby chic' effect.

Below: The distressed looking chest of drawers shown below appears to be an old piece of furniture that has enjoyed a great deal of use over the years. In fact it has been transformed from a new pine chest using a variety of 'antique' paint and glazing effects.

Interestingly, a slightly damaged or distressed looking item does not always make it less desirable. An old country dresser, for example, can be more valuable with its original but distressed paintwork still in place rather than if the paint had been stripped off. Due to the appeal of the antique look, many painters and decorators have devised imaginative techniques to produce the aged look instantly.

A combination of artist's oil paints, transparent oil glaze and white spirit when painted onto wood creates a dark appearance that simulates the natural build-up of dirt. The clever positioning of the glaze in areas where dirt usually appears produces an authentic look.

The technique of spattering glaze over furniture or wood creates tiny dark spots that look like the wood has been attacked by woodworm or other insect infestation. Rubbing paintwork with sandpaper or wire wool will remove some of the paint and make it appear lighter. This gives the appearance that the paint has faded over time from exposure to bright sunlight.

MATERIALS
Lint-free rag | White spirit | Sandpaper | Dust sheet | Rust-red and mid-blue milk paint | 3 standard decorator's brushes | Small artist's brush | Clear or tinted furniture wax | Paint stripper gun | Razor blades | Matte and satin clear polyurethane varnishes | transparent oil (scumble glaze) | Artist's oils in raw umber and black | Grade 00 wire wool | Rottenstone (fine limestone powder) |

1. ANTIQUING A CHEST OF DRAWERS
A pine chest can be transformed into an antique looking piece of furniture using various paint effects shown over the following pages. Flaking paint that is often seen on old furniture, as a result of moisture or humidity in the wood, can be recreated by applying patches of wax over an undercoat. Any subsequent coats of paint applied over the wax will not adhere to it and can be rubbed to create a flaking paint effect.
Adding a dusty finish to the chest will also help to age it. This can be done by rubbing a fine limestone powder over a glaze and then brushing off the excess. An alternative way of producing a dusty effect is to spatter a glaze over the painted surface, which produces a rustic speckled effect.

2. PAINTS AND VARNISHES
These have a tendency to craze, producing cracks in the surface of the wood. This occurs due to the wood expanding and contracting over time because of fluctuating temperatures. The 'craquelure' method, produced in France in the 18th century, replicates the cracked look. The method involves applying two coats of crackle varnish over a painted surface. The second coat is applied roughly an hour after the first and because the first coat has already started to dry, it contracts and forces the second coat to split. This causes tiny cracks to appear. When the glaze is dry, a tinted varnish is painted over the top, which settles in the cracks consequently defining them and giving the crazed effect.

3. MILK PAINTS HAVE BEEN USED for thousands of years from early cave paintings to the ancient Egyptians. Paint was originally made by mixing milk, lime and earth pigments. Over time, people added milk protein (casein) to the mix to produce a more durable paint. Milk paints offer the decorator the chance to create an aged paint effect when painted on wood and they are used in the project on the following pages. Milk paints can be bought from specialist suppliers that come already mixed. If you would like to create a particular colour yourself you can mix your own paint by adding artist's powder pigments to white casein milk paint powder.

4. CLEAN THE CHEST
Place a dust sheet beneath the chest. Begin by cleaning any dirt, grease or grime from the chest of drawers using a clean, lint-free cloth and white spirit. If the wood is bare, prepare it with a primer coat and allow to dry. If the wood has been painted or varnished in the past, use a piece of medium-grade sandpaper and rub over the surface. Once the chest is clean and dry, apply two coats of rust-red milk paint using a standard decorator's paintbrush. Leave each coat of paint to dry for 12 hours.

5. CREATING A 'WEAR AND TEAR' EFFECT
For a realistic and distressed look, add a little furniture wax dissolved in white spirit to areas where you would expect to see a little damage, such as the top and bottom of the chest, handles and on drawer fronts. Apply the wax with a decorator's brush in a thin layer. This will make the top coat bubble and flake off. Allow the wax to dry completely.

6. PAINT THE TOPCOAT
Now apply two coats of mid-blue milk paint using a decorator's paintbrush. Let each coat dry before proceeding with the next. If after applying the second coat you can still see the red basecoat showing through, you may need to apply a third coat of blue paint. Do not worry too much about achieving a perfect paint finish as you will be distressing the top coat later.

7. USE A PAINT STRIPPER GUN
Make sure that the blue paint is completely dry before continuing. Using a paint stripper gun, point it around 15cm (6in) away from the chest of drawers over the areas you previously added the wax. The paint will blister and bubble up and come away from the red basecoat. Now move on to the next step before the paint cools and the bubbles disappear.

8. FLAKING PAINT
Scrape a safety-back razor, held square-on the surface of the chest, backwards and forwards over the blistered paint. This will make the blue topcoat paint flake off, revealing the red basecoat beneath. On a few sections apply more pressure with the razor blade to remove some of the red paint to reveal the bare wood. Expose the wood in areas only where damage might occur naturally. Continue distressing the chest. Use an artist's brush and red paint to fill in any unwanted bare wood areas.

9. SMOOTH THE SURFACE
Gently rub a medium-grade sandpaper over the distressed areas you have just created. This helps to blend and smooth the raised paint edges into the surrounding finish.

The sandpaper also removes some of the blue paint so that they look slightly faded. This recreates the natural fade of painted furniture that is exposed to sunlight over long periods of time. Once you are happy with the amount of distressed paint on the chest you can protect the finish with a coat of clear matter or satin polyurethane varnish mixed in a ration of 1:1. Alternatively you can also add some more antique effects by following the next three steps.

10. CREATE A DIRTY APPEARANCE

To age your chest further you can add 'dirt' patches to make it look like it has been used a lot over the years. While the tinted glaze (top, right) is still wet, use grade 00 wire wool and rub it over the surface to redistribute the glaze and produce darker areas. It will look more realistic if you rub the wire wool around the handles or knobs and other areas where real grime might usually appear.

11. TINTED GLAZE

To make the glaze, thin one cup of transparent oil glaze or scumble glaze with white spirit in a ratio of 3:1. Then add a small amount of raw umber and black artist's oils. This will make the translucent mixture darker. Beginning at the back of one of the sides, use a decorator's brush to paint the tinted glaze over the surface. If the glaze is too light, simply add a little more of the artist's oils. If it is too dark, add more scumble and white spirit.

12. MAKE THE CHEST LOOK DUSTY

Before the glaze dries completely and while it is still tacky after using the wire wool, sprinkle some gray rottenstone powder on a lint-free cloth. Gently rub the cloth over the chest where dust might naturally gather, such as on horizontal surfaces. As the glaze is a little sticky, the powder will stick to it giving a dusty appearance. When the glaze has dried, brush any excess powder off the chest with a cloth.

THE FINISHED CHEST

Your original pine chest of drawers is finished and should look as though it has aged authentically through years of exposure to sunlight, dirt, moisture and everyday wear and tear.

MARBLING

Marble pillars or columns are often associated with ancient Greek and Roman buildings and they evoke feelings of opulence and splendor. You can make your own faux marble column by following these steps. The paint technique can also be applied to skirting boards and wall panels.

Below: The wall panels shown below are actually the result of the paint techniques described on the following pages. Marbling can transform a simple surface or object so it can be a useful skill to acquire when looking for a period effect.

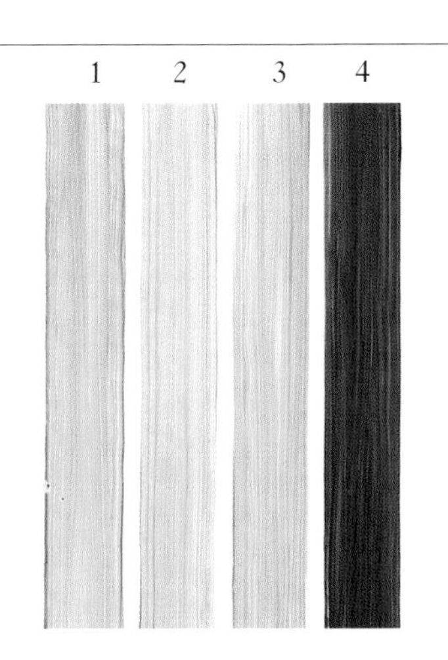

PAINTS & GLAZES

You will need to mix four different glazes for this project. Below is a list of the materials you will need to make them.

1 Artist's oils: 3 parts raw umber, 3 parts black, 2 parts veridian. Medium: 3 parts transparent oil glaze, 2 parts white spirit. Ratios in glaze: 1 part pigments, 30 parts medium.

2 The same as glaze 1 but add 1/4 part raw sienna artist's oil.

3 The same as glaze 1 but add1/4 part more veridian and 1/4 part black artist's oils.

4 Artist's oils: 2 parts raw umber, 2 parts black, 1 part veridian. Medium: 2 parts transparent oil glaze, 1 part white spirit. Ratios in glaze: 1 part pigments, 7 parts medium

Marble has been a favourite material for building and decorative purposes for centuries as it not only looks beautiful it is also a prestigious, solid and hard-wearing stone. However, due to the costs involved in quarrying and producing the stone, it is an expensive material to work with and so faux marbling techniques have been created to achieve the look without the price tag. The Renaissance first saw the emergence of marbling and the techniques have been practised ever since.

The colourful mineral deposits set within marble produce a variety of different finishes, such as hints of gleaming turquoise, quartz and opal. Decorative painters have been influenced by nature and have created different coloured marbling. Black and gold looks very striking while vibrant orange with pale brown veins running through it is just as attractive.

1. PRIME THE COLUMN Start by priming the object (here, a column) that you are going to paint and then apply an undercoat. Leave for 24 hours between coats and then add two coats of white eggshell paint. Glaze 1 is then applied by dabbing and dotting the bristle tips of a 5cm (2in) decorator's brush rapidly over the column (stippling). It is useful to look at a piece of natural marble in order to achieve an authentic pattern. The stippling should form the primary veins of the marble. Where you place these veins is up to you but be aware that the areas that do not have any primary veins will be filled with the secondary marble veins.

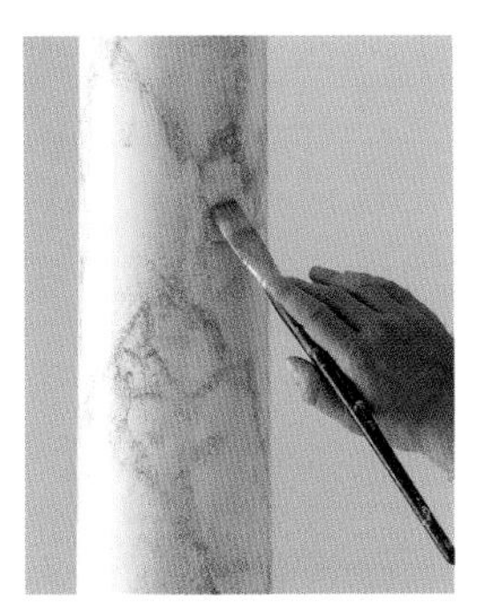

2. FORM IRREGULAR-SHAPED LINKS Take a 2cm (¾in) flat-bristled artist's brush and using the tips of the bristles, gently push the primary glaze into irregular-shaped links. Again, have a look at a real piece of marble to make sure that you form the correct shapes. Try practising on a rough piece of wood if you do not feel confident enough to work straight on to the column.

MATERIALS

Column | Primer/undercoat | 5cm (2in), 4cm (11/2in), 2.5cm (1in) decorator's brushes | White eggshell paint | 2cm (3/4in) flat-bristled artist's brush | Soft bristled jamb duster brush | Badger softener brush | Clean rag | Satin or gloss clear polyurethane varnish | Furniture wax |

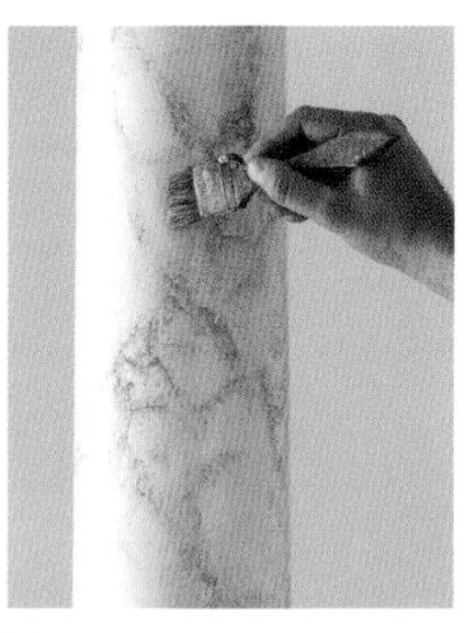

3. CREATE THE SECONDARY MARBLING VEINS Using the same stippling method as in the previous step, create the lighter, secondary veins on the column. This should be done using a 4cm (1½in) standard decorator's brush. These lines should be slightly fainter than the first set of veins.

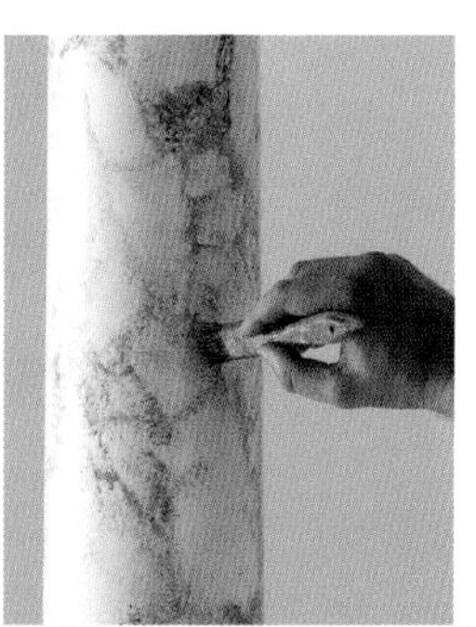

4. ADD THE COLOURED GLAZES Now it is time to add the pale green (2) and pale yellow (3) glazes. See the materials box on page 129 for the quantities needed to make each glaze. Dip the bristles of a 2.5cm (1in) decorator's brush into each glaze alternately and use the stippling technique to apply areas of colour around the edges of the primary veins.

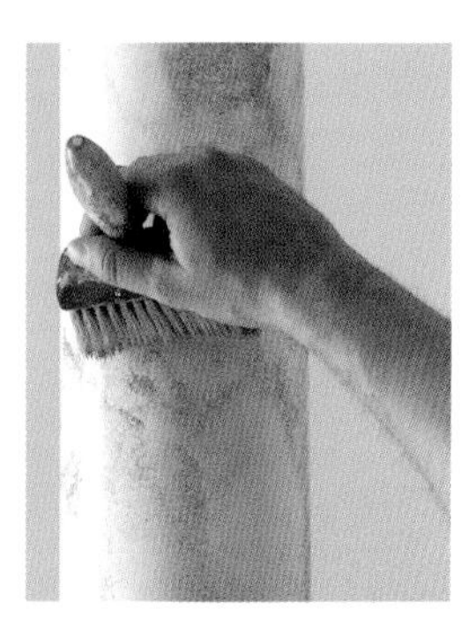

5. REMOVE THE BRUSH MARKS Next, using a soft-bristled jamb duster brush, lightly stipple over the wet glazes in order to get rid of any obvious brush marks that appear on the column.

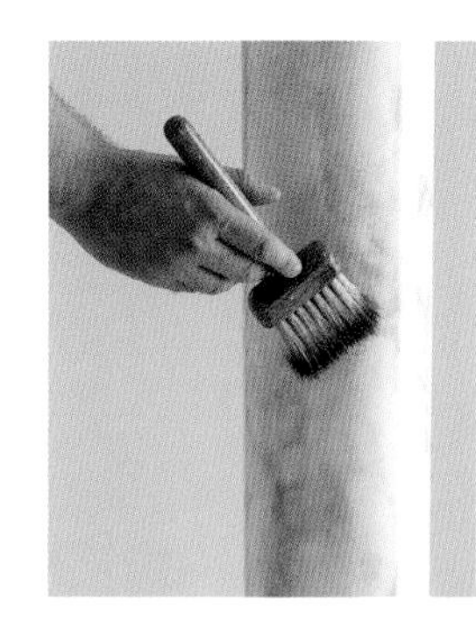

6. BLEND THE VEINS Using a badger softener brush, gently flick the bristle tips over the glazes so that the primary and secondary glazes blend together. Leave the column to dry for 24 hours.

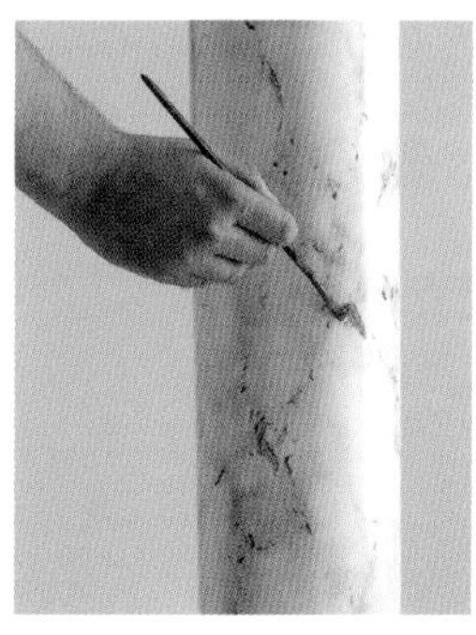

7. ADD MORE MARBLE PATTERNS Once the glazes are completely dry, use a clean rag to apply a thin coat of transparent oil glaze to the column. Then, with a small flat-bristled artist's paintbrush, apply glaze 4 in different and random shapes to give the appearance of mineral deposits within the marble. Look at a sample piece of marble or a photograph to see how the mineral deposits are formed. Most deposits follow the same paths as the primary veins but a few appear alongside the secondary veins.

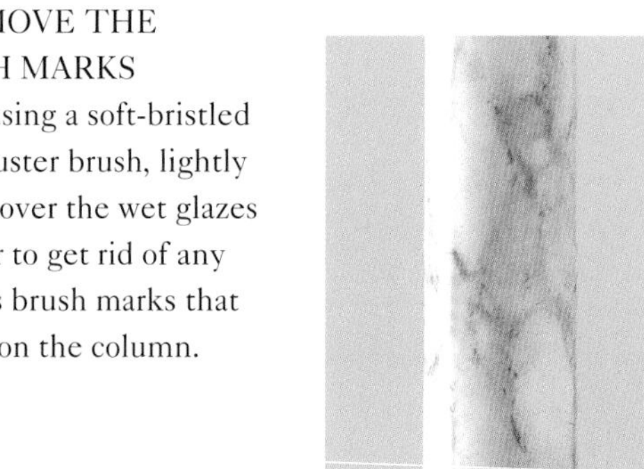

8. SOFTEN AND BLEND As soon as you have finished adding the mineral deposits and you are happy with them, lightly soften the edges of the glazes with a badger softener brush. This should be done immediately so that the glazes do not dry becoming immovable.

9. FINISHING TOUCHES

Once you have finished painting the whole column, repeat all of the steps on the base and top. Allow the glazes to dry. Then apply one or two coats of gloss or satin clear polyurethane varnish depending on how much sheen you want. Lastly, when the varnish is dry, give the column a polish using furniture wax for a gleaming finish.

Below and right: *the inner panel shown below and the finished column to the right both demonstrate how effective this technique can be. Keep practising and you will quickly become an expert!*

GILDING

Above: You can make newly repaired gilding look older by rubbing in a tinted furniture wax, or even brown shoe polish with a clean soft, lint-free cloth. For a distressed finish, apply the wax or polish with a grade-000 wire wool – very gently. Buff to a lustrous shine before removing any tape and paper from the glass.

Gilded mirror or picture frames commonly suffer minor damage, resulting from knocks and scrapes. Whatever the degree of damage to old, rare or valuable frames, it is advisable to have these repaired professionally.

At the very least, some of the gilding is usually rubbed away, but in some instances the gesso mouldings of the frame will be chipped or cracked as well. Simple mouldings can be shaped by hand before you gild, but more intricate repairs will require a cast. To do this, make a copy from an adjacent undamaged section of the moulding: using a small artist's brush, apply latex epoxy putty to a matching length of the pattern. When the latex is fully hard, peel it off carefully and fill this mould with epoxy-resin glue. When the glue is hard, peel the latex mould off the cast. Grind the new section to the correct size, fit in place and attach with epoxy resin.

A restorer may use gold leaf for the regilding, but for less-valuable frames, gold metallic powders will suffice. If only a small section requires repair, blend the new into the old by burnishing as described in the final step opposite, and then antiquing it to the correct degree with tinted furniture wax or even brown shoe polish (see caption, left).

Before you commence your repair, clean the frame thoroughly. Remove the dust with a soft-bristled dusting brush, then wash off any dirt using a soft, lint-free cloth that has been dampened with a weak solution of mild soap and lukewarm water. Be sure to pat dry immediately with terry towelling since water on the frame may soften the gesso.

Protect the glass by covering it with a large sheet of brown paper attached with masking tape stuck right up to the edge of the glass.

MATERIALS

Soft-bristled dusting brush | Soft, lint-free cotton rag |Mild liquid soap | Lukewarm water | Terry towelling rags | Large sheet of brown craft paper | Masking tape | Premixed gesso paste | Table knife | Utility of craft knife | Sandpaper, fine grade | Small artist's brush, latex, epoxy putty and epoxy resin glue (only for repairs to intricate mouldings) | Wire wool, grades 0 and 000 | Two paint brushes, 2.5–5cm wide | Artist's oil paint (burnt sienna) | White spirit | Gold metallic powder | Liquid gold size | Plastic goggles and face mask | Small saucer | Small artist's hog's-hair brush | Soft-bristled make-up brush | Tinted furniture wax or mid- or dark-brown shoe polish |

1. REPAIR THE FRAME
Small holes and cracks in the frame, such as the ones around this frame corner, are filled with premixed gesso paste. Use the blade of an old table knife to press the paste into them and build the paste up so it stands slightly proud of the old level of each crack or hole. Allow it to dry for 2 days, then make it match the profile of the surround by shaping and smoothing the dry repair, by means of a combination of fine sandpaper, needle files and a utility knife.

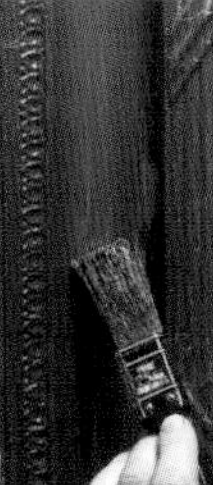

2. PAINT THE FRAME
Rub the surface of the frame down lightly with grade-0 wire wool to key the surface for oil paint. Slightly thin some burnt sienna oil paint with one or two drops of white spirit and, using a 2.5–5cm paint brush, depending on the size of your frame, apply a coat to the frame. Leave it to dry for at least 24 hours, then apply a second coat.

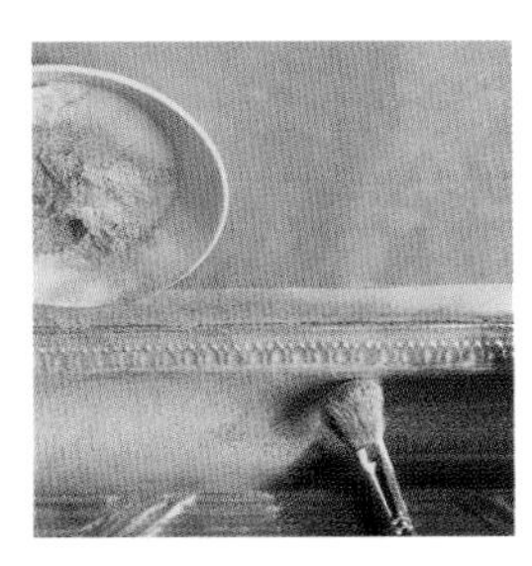

3. APPLY METALLIC POWDER
Match the original gilding to the correct shade of gold metallic powder, which is available from artist's suppliers. With your second paint brush, apply liquid gold size to the frame, making sure you cover it completely. Wait half an hour until the size is ready (sticky), then don goggles and a mask to protect your eyes, nose and mouth, and decant some metallic powder into a saucer. As soon as the size is sticky, dip the tips of the bristles of a small artist's hog's-hair brush into the powder and stipple it onto the liquid gold size. You need to work quickly, and you also need to ensure that you cover the whole frame.

4. REMOVE EXCESS POWDER
Leave the frame to dry for a minimum of 8 hours. This allows the bond between the powder and the drying liquid gold size to form fully. When dry, use a soft-bristled make-up brush to lightly dust off any powder that has not adhered to the size. If there are patches where the powder has not stuck, you will need to repeat steps 2 and 3.

5. BURNISH NEW GILDING
From a fist-sized piece of soft, lint-free cotton rag, make a flat pad. Gently rub it back and forth over the gilding to burnish it. Expect some powder to come off on the pad, and re-form it for a fresh surface or even replace it if necessary. If you like the gilding bright and new-looking, stop here. To give the frame an attractively worn appearance, you can rub quite hard in places, which will allow the burnt sienna ground colour to show through, albeit indistinctly. To age your item further, follow the instructions in the caption on the opposite page.

STENCILLING

Stencilling is the transfer of a pattern or design onto a background by applying contrasting colour through cut-outs in a stencil card. The Chinese are credited with inventing the technique around 3000BCE, and ancient surviving examples of the art are to be found in other parts of the world such as Egypt. In later years, particularly in rural communities, stencilling on the walls, a form of folk art, was a relatively cheap way introducing colour and pattern into the home and imitating the wallpapered interiors of wealthier urban homes.

The versatility and simplicity of stencilling has ensured its survival and seen it flourish as a decorative technique from the late 19th century until now. It played an important role in the work of the artists as diverse as William Morris and Charles Rennie Mackintosh – our example mimics the style of the stencilled wall panels in his tea rooms in Glasgow.

Happily for would-be stencillers today, an enormous range of pre-cut stencils is available. If you don't find anything you like, choose your motif from (non-copyright) reference material and re-size it using a photocopier with a reduce/enlarge facility if you need to. Of course, you can draw it freehand if you prefer. Trace the design onto a piece of stencil card (available from most good craft stores), then tape the card to a cutting board with masking tape. Carefully cut the design out with a craft knife. When cutting a curve, slowly turn the card around the blade rather than the blade around the card, to reduce the risk of the blade slipping.

***Above:** Charles Rennie Mackintosh was trained as an architect but he is perhaps better known today for the beautiful design and stencil work (such as shown above) that he used in the decorative schemes he designed for the buildings on which he worked.*

MATERIALS

Reference material | Photocopier | Tracing paper | Masking tape | Pencil | Stencil card | Cutting board | Craft knife | Ruler | Spirit level | Small mixing containers | Transparent oil (scumble) glaze | White spirit | Artist's oils or milk paints in chosen colours | Stencil brushes and/or marine sponges | Eraser | Lining paper | Lint-free rag | Sandpaper |

1. TAPE YOUR STENCIL

With low-tack masking tape, position the stencil and tape it in place. If you are working directly onto the wall and not in a frame such as this, stand well back to establish the right height before you attach the stencil. Make a series of fine pencil lines to mark the position of the base of the stencil card for the whole of the run you are planning. When you are ready to tape, check that the card is straight, both vertically and horizontally, with a spirit level.

2. APPLY THE FIRST COLOUR

Start by painting the motif of the largest single colour, in this example, the pink rose blooms. Place a manageable amount of paint in a container such as a saucer. Dip a marine sponge into the paint, dabbing it onto lining paper to remove any excess (if you don't do this, the paint might run down the back of the paper). Gently dab the appropriate bit of the stencil – here the rose blooms. You can create subtle shadows and highlights of colour by building up layers of paint, diluting the paint or diluting the paint with a bit of water. You could apply the paint with a brush if you find that easier to use.

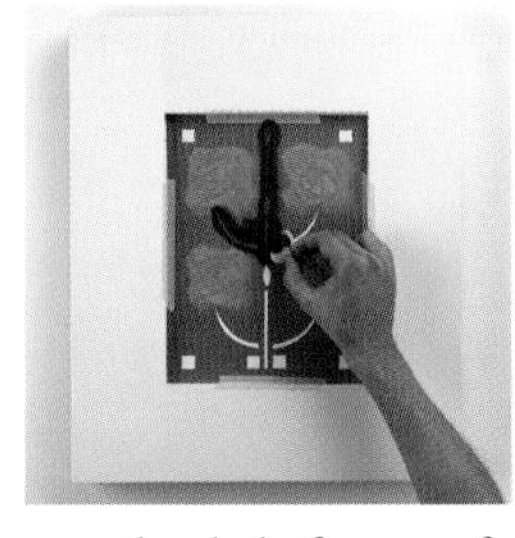

3. ADD THE SECOND COLOUR

When you have finished the pink roses, you can paint the black stems (or whatever your chosen second colour is). Allow the first colour to dry completely before carefully removing the stencil and cleaning off any smears that may have found their way onto the back of it with a damp lint-free rag. Carefully re-attach the stencil in exactly the right place and apply the second paint colour in the same way as for the first colour.

4. FINISHING TOUCHES

Complete all the details in the stencil. This is a simple design but if yours is more complicated, you may wish to add details such as shadows with a fine paint brush to lend a three-dimensional quality to the finished stencil. You may even wish to age the appearance of your stencil by rubbing it very gently with a fine- to medium-grade sandpaper (depending on the paint used).

5. THE FINISHED IMAGE

If any marks remain, clean them off with a damp cloth. When fully dried, mount and frame your print or use it in your decorating scheme as planned.

Above: Decoupage is a popular technique amongst crafters but can equally be used for larger objects such as furniture or wall effects.

PRINT EFFECT

There are an enormous number of paint and print effects that you can use to add your own individual touch to wall decoration or furniture. One that can easily be borrowed from the skills commonly used by craft enthusiasts is decoupage, which is the art of decorating and object by gluing paper cut-outs onto another surface and often then adding further embellishment to the effect by adding hand-painting or gold leaf.

Typically, small items of furniture or portable objects such as boxes or picture frames are covered by chosen cut-outs from newspapers or wrapping paper, with each layer then covered in varnishes (sometimes several coats) until the 'stuck-on' effect disappears and the final result looks more like a painted image or something that has been inlaid.

In 18th-century England, the technique of Japanning evolved, in which 30-40 layers of varnish were added to an object and then sanded to a polished finish. This finish was used to great effect on both furniture and interior decorations and became high fashion in society of the time. An example of a Japanned table can be seen at the bottom left of the opposite page.

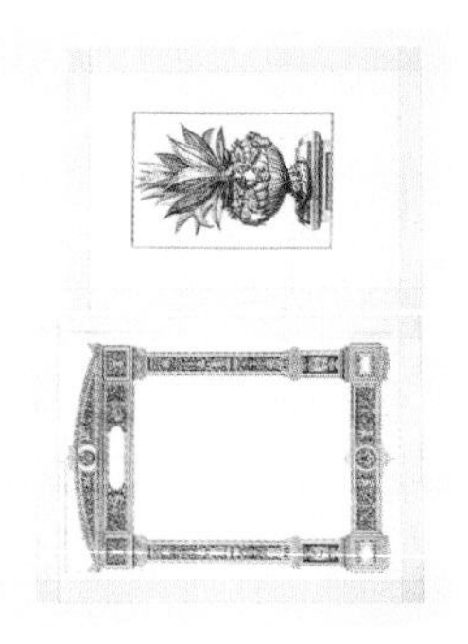

1. PHOTOCOPY A ITEM SUCH AS A PRINT AND BORDER
Using a photocopier that can reduce and enlarge, copy your chosen item onto separate pieces of good-quality paper. Re-size the originals as appropriate using the reduce/enlarge facility on the photocopier, then tape them carefully with masking tape to a flat surface such as a cutting board.

2. TINT THE PAPER
Cold tea and coffee are used to achieve this. Make several strengths of both, allow them to cool, then experiment on the same grade of paper so that you get the exact shades you want. When you are satisfied with the colour/s, then brush the liquid out over both pieces of paper. In this example, a paler brew has been chosen for the print and a darker one for the border for enhanced interest.

3. STICK BORDER/S TO THE WALL
Once the paper has dried properly, carefully remove the masking tape from the border pages. Using a small paint brush, apply a thin layer of PVA white glue to the whole of the back of the paper and stick it to the wall. Repeat for all pages and leave to dry completely.

4. ADD THE PRINTS
Measuring meticulously, mark and cut out the print/s using a craft knife and straight edge. Next, spread with PVA glue as for the borders, and very carefully stick them into position within their respective borders on the wall.

5. APPLY PROTECTIVE VARNISH
It is particularly important to protect the prints with a layer of polyurethane varnish if they are likely to be exposed to moisture or possible wear and tear in a high-traffic thoroughfare. Once the glue has dried thoroughly, apply a coat of matte or satin polyurethane varnish over the surface, paying particular care to the edges. Alternatively, follow the instructions in step 6 below for an aged effect.

6. OPTIONAL ANTIQUE EFFECT
If you wish to create an aged effect instead, make an antiquing wash with 1 part Pigment and 40 parts Medium, where the Pigment is artist's oils (3 parts burnt umber and 1 part black) and the Medium is 3 parts transparent oil glaze and 2 parts white spirit. Brush the wash over the print/s and border/s or, for a better overall finish which reduces contrast between the prints and the background, Brush the antique wash over the entire surface.

MATERIALS
Print Directory | Good-quality paper | Photocopier | Tape measure | Masking tape | Cutting board | Tea or coffee | Paint brushes of various sizes | PVA white glue | Craft knife | Pencil | Straight edge | Polyurethane varnish (matte or satin) | Optional Antiquing wash: artist's oils (burnt umber and black), transparent glaze oil and white spirit |

Below: Although more often used on small objects, tortoiseshell effect can be highly effective when used on walls and borders, as below.

TORTOISESHELL EFFECT

The original source of tortoiseshell came from the shell of sea turtles, which are now an endangered species. It is believed that tortoiseshell was introduced to Europe from the East via merchants trading with the East India Company. The colourful shells were often used as a veneer laid over wood furniture or as an inlay for ornamental objects. Tortoiseshell comes in a different colours and patterns, such as brown and yellow or red and black. The mottled patterns include stripes, spots and speckled designs.

Due to its aesthetic appeal, real tortoiseshell has been used to make stylish ornaments and furniture for centuries. However, because of the decreasing numbers of turtles in the oceans and the high cost of using real tortoise shells, the beautiful shell patterns had to be recreated in an affordable, turtle-friendly way. Skilled tortoiseshell painters emerged during the 18th century to simulate the real thing in paint.

Although, as in the room on the left, the tortoiseshell effect works well on large items, it will probably look best on smaller objects, such as trinket boxes or picture frames as the result appears more realistic.

1. PREPARE THE FRAME Before painting on your picture frame, prepare it by applying a primer or undercoat. When dry, paint two coats of black oil paint on the moulding (the raised inner and outer perimeters of the frame). Allow the paint to dry for around 24 hours after each coat of paint. Then apply two coats of paint 1 (see materials box) to the section in between.

2. ADD SCUMBLE GLAZE On one edge of the frame, apply a thin layer of scumble glaze over the yellow painted section, using a clean cotton rag.

3. DIVIDE THE FRAME Using a triangular set square, divide the yellow frame edges into equal sections and mark with a pencil line. The length of each section will obviously depend on the size of the frame you are using. Then draw a pencil line to mark the four diagonal corners.

4. APPLY RANDOM PATCHES Paint glaze 2 using a small artist's brush over the yellow part of the frame you have just applied the scumble glaze to. The shapes should be irregular and positioned randomly (see picture above or a piece of real tortoiseshell). Take care not paint over the pencil marks you made earlier.

5. CREATE TEXTURE Paint glaze 3 in the same way as glaze 2, and overlap the two colours. Now paint a few spots of glaze 4 over the two paler brown colours. Vary the number of spots, sizes and shapes to create a textured look. Next, using a badger softener brush, lightly flick the bristles over the three glaze colours to blend them. Repeat the previous steps to complete the other three sides of the frame. Leave the frame to dry for 24 hours.

6. USE DIFFERENT PAINT COLOURS To produce a red and black tortoiseshell paint effect, apply red eggshell in paint 1 and slightly increase the percentage of medium in glazes 2 and 3. Also, increase the amount of black pigment used in glaze 4. Replicate lines of ivory inserts that divide the frame by using a small artist's brush and white enamel paint.
Carefully paint over the pencil lines you made earlier using a straight edge as a guide.

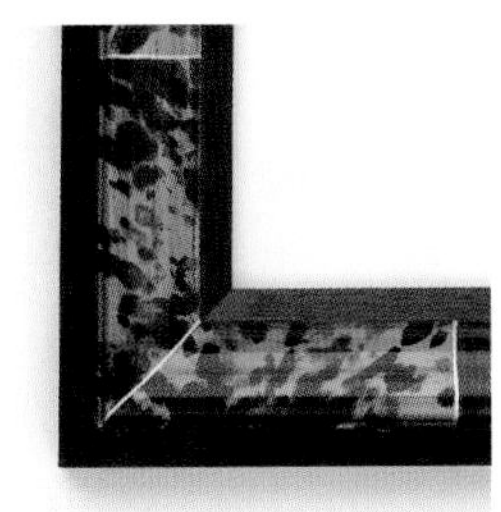

7. VARNISH THE FRAME Apply a coat of clear gloss varnish over the patterned edges but not the inner and outer dark brown edges. This will give the tortoiseshell pattern a glossy sheen. Let the varnish dry completely, which should take around 24 hours.

MATERIALS
4 x paints and glazes made up from: 1 Yellow eggshell paint | 2 Artist's oil: burnt sienna. Medium: 1 part scumble glaze, 1 part white spirit. Ratios in glaze: 1 part artist's oil, 3 parts medium | 3 Artist's oil: burnt umber. Medium: as paint 2. Ratios in glaze: as paint 2 | 4 Artist's oil: black. Medium: as paint 2. Ratios in glaze: as paint 2 | Primer/undercoat | Paintbrushes | Set square | Pencil | Clean rag | Scumble glaze | Small artist's brush | Small badger softener brush | Clear gloss polyurethane varnish | White enamel paint |

KNOW YOUR STYLE

GEORGIAN

The Georgian era was long. Technically it spanned the period from 1714, when George I came to the throne, to 1830, when George IV died. However, in design terms it generally means the period from 1714 until around 1800, when Regency style became prevalent (see p.150). The reigns of George I and George II (1714–1760) are referred to as the early Georgian period, and the first four decades of the reign of George III as the late Georgian period. The taste for Baroque style persisted into the early 18th century, and fashions

Previous pages: This elegant interior exemplifies Art Deco style, featuring typical period details and furniture.

Opposite: A set of fine Chippendale chairs sit around an extending mahogany table in this grand Georgian dining room that also includes an inlaid sideboard displaying Georgian and Victorian silver and glass.

for Rococo, chinoiserie, and Japanese silks and lacquerware had strong appeal. But the enduring influence of the era was the Classical architecture of ancient Rome and Greece, which inspired Neo-classical style in buildings and interiors of the time.

In the 18th century, wealthy young men were sent on the Grand Tour of Europe to finish their education and visit a trail of Classical sites. They returned weighed down by paintings, furniture, and objets d'art and with their heads full of inspiration and ideas about Classical style.

In tandem, a new generation of British architects emerged who were galvanized by the writings and designs of Andrea Palladio, a 16th-century Italian architect who revived interest in the buildings of ancient Rome. The Palladian Revival dominated the architecture of the early Georgian period, led by Lord Burlington, Colen Campbell, William Kent, and, later, Sir William Chambers. The Neo-classicism of architects such as Robert Adam and Sir John Soane prevailed in the late Georgian era. Georgian domestic architecture thus featured pedimented front doorcases leading into well-proportioned, light-filled rooms with deep windows.

In the early Georgian period, rooms tended to be lined with pine panelling painted in soft, muted colours such as off-whites, greys, stone, and sage green – a palette limited by the pigments available. Mantelpieces over fireplaces became wider to make room for the growing choice of ornaments such as ceramics, figurines, and clocks.

INSPIRATIONAL INTERIOR

An extraordinary tribute to 18th-century living, Dennis Severs' house at 18 Folgate Street in Spitalfields, London, was the creation of the late Dennis Severs, an artist who died in 1999. Severs lived in the house just as the original occupants, Huguenot silk weavers, might have. He even created an imaginary family, the Jervises, to share it with. Now regularly open to the public, the house pulsates with the historic atmosphere he created. Tiptoe through rooms lit by candlelight to inspect the furnishings and collections.

Although not strictly Georgian in style, this house offers a unique view into an 18th-19th century home.

GEORGIAN ANTIQUES

The Georgian style is predominantly associated with furniture, although it is also evident in the silverware, glassware, and ceramics of the time. What is striking about the furniture is a lack of abundant surface decoration – the emphasis being on the beauty of the wood itself. When looking at Georgian furniture, it is important to remember that the style spanned almost a century, during which it developed significantly.

Early Georgian pieces (c.1714–60) are typically made from walnut and reflect the Rococo style that was popular in France at the same time, albeit with far more restraint (see p.146). Look for elegant, gently curved cabriole legs with scrolled or claw-and-ball feet on small pieces such as chairs and card tables. The scallop shell motif was a common feature and might be found on the knees of chair and table legs or on the aprons of large storage pieces. One area in which early Georgian furniture did emulate that of France was in the occasional elaborately carved and gilded piece – usually the reserve of fanciful girandoles (mirrors).

Late Georgian pieces (c.1760–1800) reflect the move toward Neo-classical design that culminated in the Regency style (see p.150). Furniture is much more architectural in style and proportion and is typically made from mahogany, often with inlays of precious metals, such as gold, silver, or bronze. Look for architectural elements such as broken pediments, moulded cornices, and pilasters.

Above: *The small size and 'flame' veneered serpentine front of this Georgian mahogany chest of drawers are amongst the factors that make it desirable.*

Below: *Low backs on 18th century sofas perhaps kept expensive upholstery away from fashionable powdered wigs. This camel–back sofa also has out–scrolled arms and square section legs with stretchers.*

DESIGN HERO

Thomas Chippendale (1718-79) brilliantly captured the spirit of the times. With tremendous foresight, he published in 1754 The Gentleman and Cabinet-Maker's Director, the first pattern book to focus on furniture alone. Available to wealthy patrons and cabinet-makers alike, the publication presented designs for chairs, tables, desks, storage pieces, and more, complete with variations that gave the client a wealth of choice. While the basic form of a piece remained the same, each was carved in such a way that it became Rococo, Chinese, Gothic, or Neo-classical in style, reflecting the fashions of the time.

Known as a Gainsborough chair, this well-carved 19th century mahogany armchair is elaborately carved and is typical of the mid–18th century Chippendale taste.

Left: *Early 18th century chests–on–chests, or 'tallboys', were typically made from walnut with feather banding, as here.*

Below: *Made in the Chippendale manner, this mahogany tripod table has a piecrust top and a cabriole pedestal with pad feet.*

ROCOCO

The exuberant and highly decorative Rococo style enjoyed its heyday between 1720 and 1760. Its roots lay in early 18th-century France, when artists and craftsmen reacted against the heavy Baroque style exemplified by the opulent Palace of Versailles. They preferred a look that was lighter and more fluid. Rococo was particularly well suited to furniture and mirrors, ceramics and silver, and became fashionable in Britain to a limited extent.

In essence the word Rococo is derived from the French word rocaille, which

Opposite, above and below: In addition to its obvious decorative exuberance, Rococo style was also about a desire for more comfort and less formality in living spaces. Women and their tastes became more influential at Court, as did conversation, games and other social pursuits. Upholstery became fashionable and, in addition to painted furniture, it was often chosen to match the interior decoration of a room.

describes the rock and shell motifs that became synonymous with the Rococo style. Other important motifs were scrolls in the shape of "S" or "C", entwining foliage, and swags of flowers. A stylized version of the acanthus mollis leaf was widely used, and mythical beings such as cherubs and mermaids were often depicted. All these motifs would feature en masse, often in asymmetrical form, to give a flowing, naturalistic appearance.

Rococo's elegant edge translated well into interior decoration. Pastel colours, white, and gold featured on walls, upholstery fabrics, and drapes, while mirrors made rooms lighter and more spacious. Craftsmanship was evident in elaborate plasterwork on walls and ceilings, and also in overmantel mirrors and picture frames carved from lime or pine and then covered in layers of gesso to make a smooth surface before painting or gilding.

Rococo became fashionable in London in the 1730s. One of the biggest names to emerge from that time is the silversmith Paul de Lamerie. The son of French Huguenots who had settled in London, he set up a workshop to make many beautiful pieces – ranging from coffee and chocolate pots to cake and bread baskets, candlesticks, wine coolers, and tureens – for his aristocratic clientele. The Victoria and Albert Museum in London has a fine collection on show.

At London's Wallace Collection, paintings by the 18th-century French artists Boucher and Fragonard capture the joie de vivre and romance of the Rococo style.

INSPIRATIONAL INTERIOR

This little beauty, a mid-18th-century Rococo pier glass and table, was perhaps collected by a member of the Hervey family on the Grand Tour, or snapped up from a dealer. Framed by silk curtains, the glass and table are situated in the airy drawing room of Ickworth in Suffolk. The Italianate palace was the Hervey family seat until the mid-20th century and illustrates the very 18th-century habit of collecting, with family portraits by Gainsborough, Huguenot silver, and Regency furniture and china.

The richly decorated curving, floral and foliate carved details on this magnificent Portuguese pier glass and table are highlighted in gilt.

FRENCH ROCOCO ANTIQUES

Central to the French rococo style are the sinuous lines and curvaceous forms that are typified by the two-drawer bombe commode and the pear- or baluster-shaped silverware and ceramics that became the height of fashion during this period. Furniture forms are generally light and feminine, yet busy with a profusion of surface ornamentation, which might include exquisite marquetry and parquetry, pretty porcelain mounts, or japanned motifs. Look out for elaborately carved, often gilded, wood on chairs and tables and beautiful gilt-brass or ormolu mounts on commodes and writing tables. Asymmetry is key to this look, seen in the elaborate C- and S-scrolls that make up much of the carving, and in the shapely cabriole legs with pad or claw-and-ball feet that define the style.

In addition to the commode, typical forms include the bonheur-du-jour (a delicate lady's writing desk), the fauteuil (an upholstered armchair with open sides), and elaborately carved and gilded mirrors and timepieces. Common motifs include carved scallop shells and rockwork, arabesques, and flower forms. Typical fabrics are satin, silk, and damask in soft, light colours – pale green and blue, lilac, pink, and yellow.

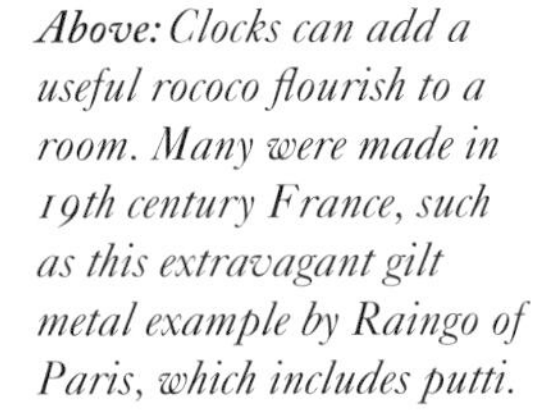

***Above:** Clocks can add a useful rococo flourish to a room. Many were made in 19th century France, such as this extravagant gilt metal example by Raingo of Paris, which includes putti.*

Silverware and ceramics are also elaborate, with scrolling, serpentine forms and asymmetrical floral or shell and rockwork imagery. Ceramics often betray the influence of the Far East with mythological chinoiserie motifs or depict idyllic garden scenes, known as fêtes champêtres, inspired by the paintings of Jean-Antoine Watteau. Sometimes painted using bright enamel colours, ceramics with gilded elements are particularly associated with the Sèvres porcelain factory.

DESIGN HERO

Cabinetmaker to Louis XIV of France, André-Charles Boulle (1642–1732) excelled at the exquisite marquetry that has since taken his name. Created using only the most exotic materials – brass, ivory, ebony, tortoiseshell – the labour-intensive process required precision cutting of the same intricate design from sheets of brass and tortoiseshell. The brass pattern was set into a tortoiseshell background and the tortoiseshell was set into a brass background. The two, known as "first-part" and "counter-part", were then used to decorate two companion pieces of furniture.

The gilt brass mounts and ornate brass scrolling decoration over rich red tortoiseshell on this 19th century writing table are typical of Boulle's work.

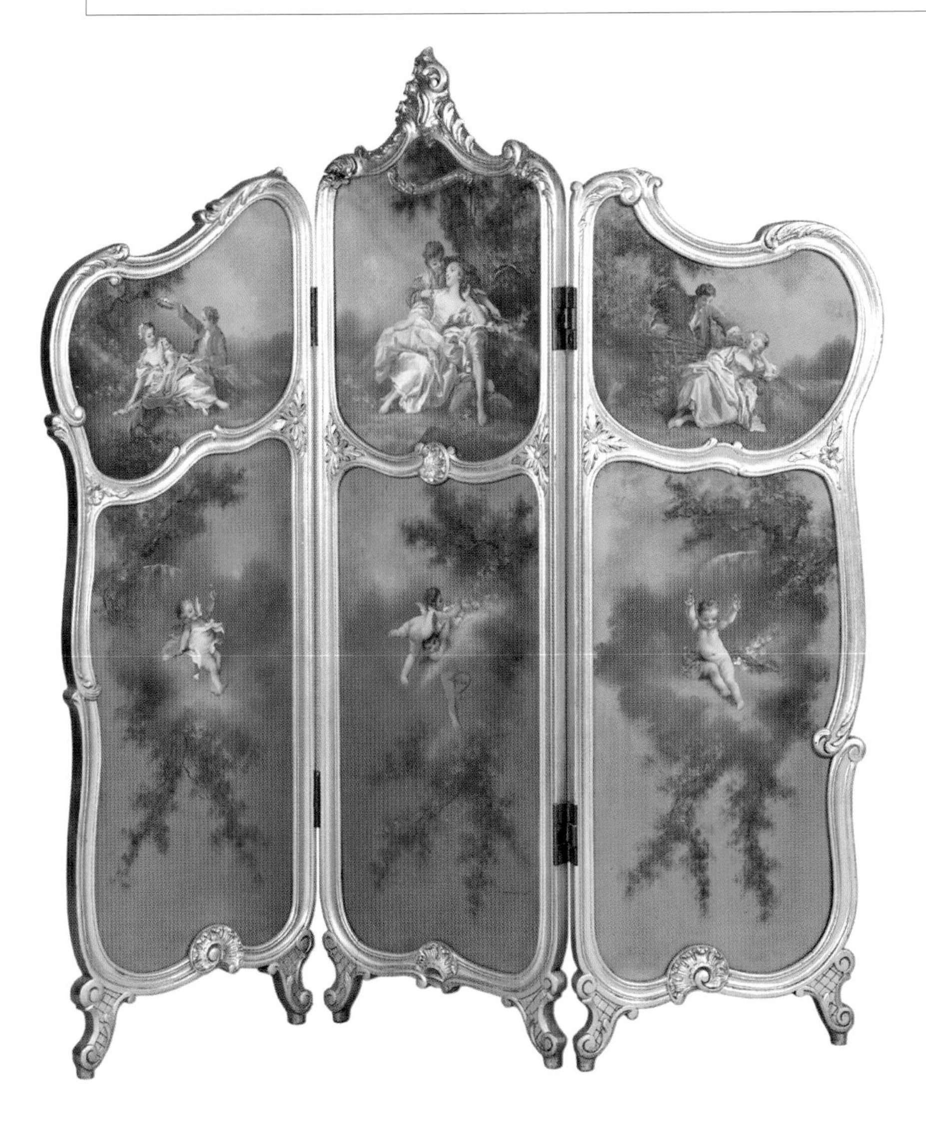

Opposite, bottom left: *Elements of this rococo giltwood pier table go against the overall symmetrical form. The auricular scroll carvings are typical of the style.*

Opposite, bottom right: *This 'Calabria' teapot was made by the French royal porcelain factory Sèvres. Dating from 1767, the floral decoration would have been very fashionable.*

Left: *The French rococo style remained popular beyond the 18th century, this giltwood and painted folding screen was made c1900. Its foliate curving frame and scenes of fête champêtres and putti are typical of the style.*

REGENCY

Regency style takes its name from the Prince of Wales, who became Regent in 1811 when his father, George III, became too ill to rule. Upon the death of his father in 1820, he reigned as George IV until his own death in 1830. Such was his influence on architecture that Regency style dominated the first three decades of the 19th century.

It was the time of Jane Austen and Napoleon Bonaparte. The Prince Regent set the tone. A great patron and collector of the arts, he decorated his London

Opposite: The Red Drawing Room at Belton House, Lincolnshire, UK. The room retains the redecorated scheme of 1810 by Sir Jeffry Wyatville. Note the Regency giltwood sofa and armchairs are Regency, which are typical of the period.

home, Carlton House on the Mall, in luxurious style. The seaside resort of Brighton became the height of fashion when in 1815 he commissioned the architect John Nash to create an Oriental-style Royal Pavilion. This pleasure-palace complex, with its domes and minarets, took seven years to complete.

The Neo-classical style continued to dominate interior decoration but became even more refined. Classical friezes featured on ceramics and wallpaper, and motifs of medals, laurel wreaths, and eagles were also popular. In furniture design, Regency Classicism emulated the style of Imperial Rome, with heavy, solid chairs, stools, and tables that featured pediments and plinths and were decorated with carved acanthus leaves, swags of flowers, and drapery.

Ceramics reflected a passion for naturalistic forms in the shape of leaves, flowers, and fruit. Greek shields, the anthemion (a stylized flower motif resembling honeysuckle), and the Greek key pattern also remained popular. These classical forms and motifs were joined by inspiration from ancient Egypt following Napoleon's campaigns there and archaeological surveys of the time, and sphinxes, hawks, and eagles were much in evidence.

By Regency times life had become a little less formal, and drawing rooms were used to entertain, play cards, write letters, sketch, and make music. Consequently, furniture became more portable and flexible with single chairs and small tables.

INSPIRATIONAL INTERIOR

The Music Room at the Royal Pavilion in Brighton is a living monument to the opulent decorating taste of the Prince Regent. Here aristocratic guests would listen to performances of music by Handel and Italian opera played by the Prince's own orchestra. The interior was designed by the high society decorator Frederick Crace, and has been re-created today according to his original plans. Lit by nine lotus-shaped chandeliers and hung with painted canvases of Chinese scenes, the effect would have been and still is pure razzle-dazzle.

Despite being ravaged by fire in 1975, and damaged by a falling minaret in 1987, the original extravagance of the music room has been fully restored.

REGENCY ANTIQUES

Top: The platform style of base, and the visual weight of this mahogany partners' table, are typical of the Regency period.

Above: Convex mirrors gave servants an all–round view of a dining room. During the Regency period, frames often bore eagles and candleholders.

Right: With its elegant lyre–shaped and splayed legs, this Regency mahogany work table is all about curves.

Antiques associated with the Regency period in Britain epitomize the Neo-classical style that dominated Europe at the time. Much of the furniture from this period has an understated elegance, with light, symmetrical forms that reveal the influence of ancient Greece and Rome. It was made predominantly from mahogany, or sometimes rosewood. You might find slender, bow-fronted side cabinets, work tables on lyre-shaped trestle supports, and tall chests of drawers or davenport desks. Many pieces have elegant reeded or fluted tapering legs and beautifully figured veneers with little additional decoration. The flair for exoticism that characterized the most prestigious Regency furniture was borne out in parcel-gilt ebonized pieces – literally stained black to make it look like ebony – and in the use of exotic veneers such as satinwood and calamander. Several designs take inspiration from ancient forms, among them the X-frame chair and the chaise longue, while seminal pieces include the Trafalgar chair – characterized by its horizontal slats and sabre legs – sofa tables with drop ends, and convex mirrors in round, giltwood frames. Motifs that you will see time and again include the Greek key, ram's head, lion's paw feet, and the classical urn shape.
The urn motif is also ubiquitous among Regency silver, glass, and ceramics, where it is particularly prevalent in pottery and glass vases, rummer wine glasses with "lemon squeezer" bases, and fine silver ewers and coffee pots.

DESIGN HERO

With remarkable intuition and an innovative curiosity, Josiah Wedgwood (1739-95) developed a range of stoneware in all manner of Neo-classical manifestations that brilliantly imitated ancient Greek and Roman forms. The best-known were black basalte, rosso antico, and jasper ware. At his factory in Staffordshire Wedgwood was the first to recognize the potential of mass production. His division of labour, by which each stage of an item's making was performed by an appropriately skilled labourer, hugely sped up the manufacturing process, enabling the production of many products for a rapidly growing and diverse market.

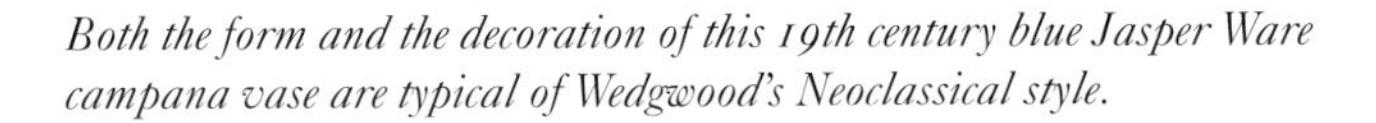

Both the form and the decoration of this 19th century blue Jasper Ware campana vase are typical of Wedgwood's Neoclassical style.

Above: *Although heavier in feel than many Georgian sofas, the curving mahogany frame, highlighted by the cream fabric, gives this Regency sofa a sculptural appearance.*

VICTORIAN

When Victoria ascended to the throne in 1837, who would have predicted that the young Queen would rule until 1901? The long era over which she presided was characterized by the rise of the British Empire and the growth of the middle classes in urban and suburban areas. Newly developed mass-manufacturing processes meant that the interior style that was once the territory of the well heeled could be aspired to and attained by ordinary people, who wanted as many home comforts as they could afford.

Opposite, above and below: Queen Victoria's reign was a time of great change in the home. Mass production meant more goods were available to buy. The newly emerging middle classes took immense pride in their homes which they saw as a reflection of status.

A prime example is that of wallpaper. Expensive block-printed papers had first become popular in the mid-18th century, but by the 1830s manufacturers had devised a way of printing continuous rolls that made it far more affordable. Flock – which had been highly fashionable in the wealthiest Georgian homes – was now widely available. It was followed later in the century by Lincrusta and Anaglypta, embossed papers that imitated stamped leather, wood panelling, and shallow stucco-work.

Tiles were another boom product. Minton developed patterned encaustic tiles in the 1830s, and by the 1860s tiles of all kinds were used everywhere, seen on front paths, in entry halls, and on fireplace surrounds. Not only were tiles decorative and available in many patterns and motifs, but they were also easy to clean in a world with muddy streets and increasingly polluted air.

The Victorians loved strong, rich decorating shades such as red, sharp yellow, and bottle green. The taste for ornamentation grew and, by the Great Exhibition of 1851 at the Crystal Palace, colour and overblown decoration were ubiquitous. Rooms were bursting with dark-stained furniture, overstuffed upholstery, fringed curtains, pot plants on stands, and ceramic ornaments such as flat-backed Staffordshire figures made expressly to stand on mantelpieces.

Of the many revivals that occurred in the Victorian period, none was more influential than the Gothic Revival, inspired by the great medieval churches and cathedrals of Europe.

INSPIRATIONAL INTERIOR

What have these walls heard? The voices of Tennyson, Dickens, and Browning, amazingly, as this drawing room was a salon for London's leading literary figures in the Victorian era. The Scottish essayist and author Thomas Carlyle rented a terraced house in the unfashionable village of Chelsea in 1834, which rapidly became a favourite haunt of writers. Now owned by the National Trust, the house has all its original contents and is a time capsule of tasteful 19th-century style.

The homely mix of styles obviously comforted Carlyle deeply – he spent his last hours in this room, dying there in February 1881.

VICTORIAN ANTIQUES

The vast majority ofVictorian antiques reflect the prevailing interest in styles from the preceding 500 years. This is primarily exhibited in the Gothic, Rococo, and Neo-classical revivals that dominate this period. Gothic revival pieces typically share similar motifs – trefoils, quartrefoils, latticework, and pointed arches – carved in solid oak furniture with little additional surface ornament.

Rococo Revival pieces include furniture, ceramics, and silverware with elaborate, often asymmetrical scrolls and rockwork designs that were first seen in early 18th-century France. Neo-classical Revival furniture forms include faithful reproductions of Georgian and Regency pieces – a late Georgian Chippendale chair or Sheraton breakfront sideboard, for example. Pieces that mix elements from different periods – say, a symmetrical Neo-classical form decorated with Gothic or Rococo-style designs – are also commonplace. Applied ornamentation and embellishment are prolific, with marquetry panels, gilt-brass mounts, porcelain mounts, enamelling, gilding, and Wedgwood plaques in abundance. Richly upholstered pieces are also plentiful, and typical forms include button-backed chairs and sofas and wingback armchairs. Seminal furniture forms from this period include the balloon-back chair and all manner of display cabinets used for housing large collections of everything from dolls to stuffed birds.

Developments in the production of ceramics saw a huge volume of blue-and-white transfer-printed dinner services, with topographical or Classical scenes. In addition to the motifs common to each of the revival styles, Victorian wares also display a fascination with designs from the far-flung cultures of China, Japan, India, and Persia. Look out for glassware and ceramics decorated with mythical creatures, arabesques, or stylized floral patterns in rich colours.

Above: Comfortable, sturdy Victorian mahogany framed button–back armchairs such as this are neither hard to find nor expensive. Bring them into the 21st century by covering them in new fabric.

Right: Reminiscent of a church or the Houses of Parliament, and possibly designed by Augustus Pugin, this early 19th century carved oak hexagonal side table is pure Gothic Revival.

Below: This 19th century Minton porcelain Rococo revival urn and cover is typical of the Victorian fashion for 'maximalism' and mixing richly decorated styles .

Above: This Victorian burr walnut breakfront credenza has an architectural form and a panelled arabesque door.

DESIGN HERO

A remarkable designer, who was in many respects ahead of his time, Dr. Christopher Dresser (1834-1904) was a firm believer in the fitness of a piece for its purpose. Influenced by Japanese art and design, Dresser designed silverware with forms that were prescient of the modernist age. He championed a more stylistic approach to design than the representational approach pioneered by William Morris. This is particularly noticeable in his stylized botanical drawings, in which he emphasizes the geometric nature of many plant forms.

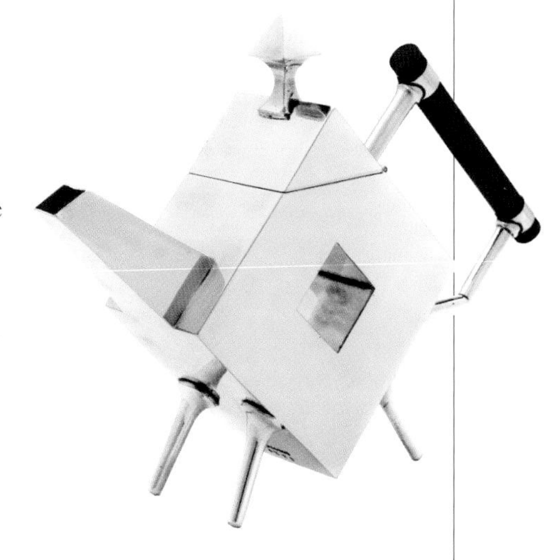

The geometric form of this James Dixon & Sons silver-plated teapot designed in 1879 by Christopher Dresser is decades ahead of its time.

ARTS AND CRAFTS

Against the backdrop of a Victorian society caught up in a wave of mass production and overblown style, the Arts and Crafts movement came to prominence in the 1860s. Founded by the artist and designer William Morris, the movement reviled mass production and espoused a return to traditional skills to produce handcrafted furniture and decorative arts that were both beautiful and useful.

For inspiration the movement drew on British vernacular styles of architecture,

Opposite, above and below: *The Arts and Crafts movement was made up of English designers and writers who wanted a return to well-made, handcrafted goods instead of mass-produced, poor quality machine-made items. The top image shows examples of period pieces and, beneath it, the influence of this style on contemporary interiors.*

furniture-making, and decorative arts. An emphasis on the natural qualities of the materials used, especially wood, was a key principle, as was simplicity of form, and very quickly the Arts and Crafts movement established an alternative to high Victorian ornamentation.

In Arts and Crafts patterns and designs, flat, stylized flowers, foliage, birds, insects, and other natural motifs were widely used. These can be seen on the textiles and wallpapers produced by Morris & Co., the company he set up in 1861 to provide Arts and Crafts wares for the home. The nub of the style can be seen today at the Red House in Bexleyheath, south-east London. Built for William Morris by Philip Webb in 1858–60, this was where Morris and other members of the Arts and Crafts movement experimented with ideas for interior decoration and furnishing.

Arts and Crafts designer, architect, and writer, C.R. Ashbee designed jewellery, silverware, and furniture. He founded the Guild of Handicraft in London's East End in 1888, moving it to Chipping Campden in the Cotswolds in 1902.

The store Liberty & Co., established in 1875 in Regent Street, London, specialized in selling work by Arts and Crafts designers and craftsmen, including ranges by the prolific designer of pewter and silverware Archibald Knox, metalware by Christopher Dresser, and ceramics by William Moorcroft. Around the turn of the century, Ambrose Heal, of Heal's furniture store, brought his own designs in the Arts and Crafts style to a wider audience.

INSPIRATIONAL INTERIOR

With glorious views over the Sussex High Weald in southern England and a 5-hectare (12-acre) hillside garden to stroll around, Standen is a treat for lovers of Arts and Crafts. It was designed and built in 1891–4 by Philip Webb, one of William Morris's closest associates, for the wealthy London solicitor James Beale. Inside you'll find all the big names of the Arts and Crafts movement. This drawing room is papered in "Sunflower" wallpaper designed by Morris and has glassware by William De Morgan and metalwork by W.A.S. Benson.

The Arts and Crafts style drawing room at Standen includes a hand-knotted rug designed by William Morris.

ARTS AND CRAFTS ANTIQUES

Central to the Arts and Crafts movement is an emphasis on handmade as opposed to machine-made goods. This was reflected in the revival of traditional craftsmanship from medieval times. Arts and Crafts furniture is therefore almost exclusively made of oak and relies on structure and construction rather than superfluous decorative detail for its appeal. Typical pieces include solid wood dressers, settles, hallstands, small tables, and simple chairs, often with rush seats. Exposed dovetail or mortise-and-tenon joints and handcrafted ironmongery, such as finely wrought hinges, are common. Motifs are minimal and take inspiration from vernacular medieval or Celtic forms, such as stylized flowers and foliage, hearts, and trefoils. The oak is often stained to make it warmer and darker in appearance, giving the impression of age and emphasizing the grain of the wood.

In addition, traditional craftsmanship is evident in other disciplines of the decorative arts. A number of art potteries were established, among them the Ruskin Pottery, whose simple forms beautifully accentuated the innovative speckled or streaked glazes that the artists developed. Arts and Crafts metalware is also significant, with repoussé-hammered copper and brass chargers, bowls, and candlesticks and hand-hammered silver tea sets and vases. Also prevalent are the "Cymric" (gold and silver) and "Tudric" (pewter) pieces designed by Archibald Knox, among others, for the prestigious Liberty & Co. shop in London. Although these were made using industrial methods, not by hand, they nevertheless epitomize the Arts and Crafts style.

Above left: *The simple lines of the form, tongue–and –groove doors, use of undecorated oak and the medieval style of the metal hinges and handles on this sideboard exemplify the Arts and Crafts style.*

Above right: *This Liberty & Co. pewter bowl, made c1905, is from the 'Tudric' range designed by Archibald Knox and was inspired by Celtic and Manx motifs and designs.*

DESIGN HERO

Credited as the father of the Arts and Crafts movement, William Morris (1834-96) established a successful company that produced a range of fine Arts and Crafts homewares. He also influenced the establishment of the medieval-style craftsmen's guilds that epitomize the period. Besides these and other achievements, Morris created textiles. Using only natural animal and vegetable dyes he produced the subtle, earthy colours that so perfectly reflected the medieval examples he sought to emulate. The soft, rich reds, blues, greens, and browns were ideal for the large-scale repeating animal and plant motifs that characterized his designs, many of which remain popular today.

The printed 'Strawberry Thief' cotton was inspired by thrushes in Morris' garden at Kelmscott Manor and was intended for use as curtains, or on walls.

Above: *William Howson Taylor's Ruskin pottery was known for its varied, complex glazes as seen on this vase from 1907.*

Right: *Vernacular motifs, such as the hearts and the tulips on the copper panel, on this Wylie & Lochhead oak hall table were frequently used in Arts and Crafts furniture.*

ART NOUVEAU

The Art Nouveau style originated in France and Belgium in the 1890s and became an international style that was adopted as far afield as the United States. The name was derived from the opening in 1895 of Samuel Bing's Parisian gallery La Maison de l'Art Nouveau, where artworks and crafts encapsulated a new, organic style rooted firmly in nature.

Art Nouveau echoes the fluidity of 18th-century Rococo style, but is simpler and more graphic. Key motifs are stylized leaves and flowers, stems, winged

Opposite, above and below: Art nouveau could be said to be the first 20th century modern style. It takes inspiration from the natural world, as can be clearly seen in the sinuous forms of the door and mirror frames of the grand assembly room shown in the top image. Art Nouveau influence can also be seen in the amazing tiled room shown below.

insects – especially the dragonfly – and the female form, dressed in billowing robes and with flowing, Pre-Raphaelite hair. These motifs were expressed in curving, energetic marks termed "whiplash lines". The colour palette was equally natural; a peacock feather has the typical colours of Art Nouveau – iridescent blues, greens, greys, purples, and pinks.

It was a dramatic style of design that characterized a genre of objects and furniture created from 1890 up until World War I. Art Nouveau translated well into glass, metalware, jewellery, furniture, architecture, and illustration. It can clearly be seen in the famous advertising posters by Alphonse Mucha and the book illustrations by the British artists Aubrey Beardsley and Walter Crane, filled with twining whiplash lines based on tendrils, stems, flowers, and leaves.

Other famous exponents include Emile Gallé, who made beautiful glass vases and bowls, and René Lalique, who created scintillating jewellery. Iridescence was another favourite Art Nouveau look, perfected by the American Louis Comfort Tiffany in his Favrile glasswares, and by the Austrian company Loetz. Architecturally, the look can be seen at many Métro stations around Paris, and in the Art Nouveau hotspot of Brussels, where over 500 original buildings still stand.

In Britain Archibald Knox became synonymous with the Art Nouveau style, producing the silver "Cymric" and pewter "Tudric" ranges of metalware for Liberty & Co. from 1899.

INSPIRATIONAL INTERIOR

Commanding fine views over the Clyde estuary, Hill House in Helensburgh, near Glasgow, is Charles Rennie Mackintosh's finest domestic design. Mackintosh had already completed his redesigned Glasgow School of Art, and had begun a series of commissions for Miss Cranston's famous Glasgow tearooms, when the Glasgow publisher Walter Blackie commissioned him in 1902 to build Hill House. Mackintosh designed the house from the inside out, including both the interior plans and elevations. The Blackie family took possession in 1904 and enjoyed not only a house and garden designed by Mackintosh, but also furniture, interior fittings, and decorating schemes.

The stylised rose in the panels and the rectilinear banister spindles are recurring motifs in Mackintosh's work.

ART NOUVEAU ANTIQUES

The dominant themes of the Art Nouveau style are reminiscent of those seen during the French Rococo period in the first half of the 18th century (see p.147). Sinuous "whiplash" curves are evident in all disciplines of the decorative arts: they appear as friezes on case furniture and as silver mounts on glassware; they are carved, etched, or sculpted as a decorative feature on smaller pieces of furniture and ceramics; or they form an integral part of a design – the arm of a chair, or the newly revived cabriole leg, for example. These curvaceous lines are ubiquitous.

Further motifs to look out for come from nature – intertwined plant stems, tendrils, leaves, flowers, and insects like the dragonfly. The female figure is also a recurring motif: nudes with long, flowing hair and diaphanous gowns frequently adorn ceramic, glass, and metal pieces.

As with Rococo furniture, forms are generally light and feminine, often made from mahogany with intricate, exotic-wood marquetry surfaces and fretwork friezes that reveal the influence of the Far East. In an attempt to emulate nature, there is a deliberate asymmetry in the decoration of many pieces and sometimes in the forms themselves. Seminal pieces include elegant display cabinets and tiered tables.

Among several innovations arising from this period were those in glassmaking. Alongside Tiffany-style stained glass and lead pieces (typically lamps), look out for etched and enamelled vases, cameo glass pieces, and iridescent glass, all of which epitomize the era.

Above: *'Zodiac', designed in 1896 by Alphonse Mucha, includes many of his most recognisable motifs such as an intricate floral border, Art Nouveau jewellery and a serene lady with a halo and curling, wavy hair.*

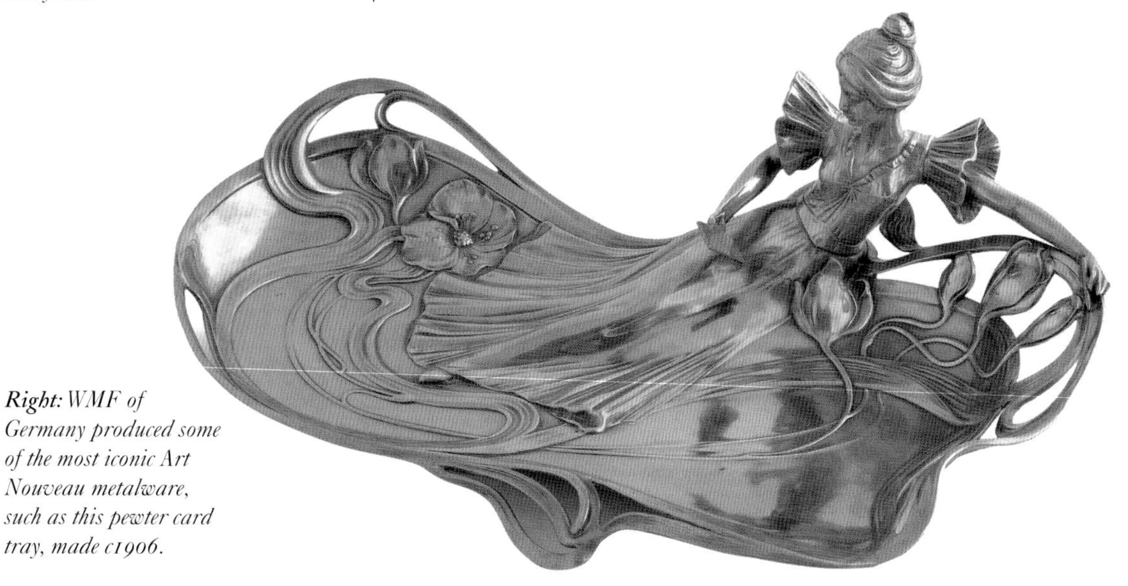

Right: *WMF of Germany produced some of the most iconic Art Nouveau metalware, such as this pewter card tray, made c1906.*

DESIGN HERO

Emile Gallé (1846-1904) was one of France's most notable and talented art nouveau designers. in 1901, he founded the influential école de Nancy, which grew to count design titans Louis Majorelle, Victor Prouvé, and the Daum brothers amongst its members. The design school and workshop were set up on the lines of English Arts and Crafts guilds, and promoted modernization of technical training in the decorative and applied arts. In addition to Symbolist literature, Gallé was inspired by the natural world around him, which provided ideas for forms as well as decoration. Flowers, vines, insects and fruit all appeared in his designs for glass and furniture.

This carved mahogany display cabinet by Gallé includes rich inlay of clematic vines.

Above: *Elegant fin de siécle ladies wearing diaphanous clothing, often blending into the sinuous curves of the form, recur in Art Nouveau designs, as seen on this spelter clock by A. De Ranieri.*

Left: *The stylised and curving floral designs of the marquetry on this mahogany display cabinet are quintessentially Art Nouveau.*

ART DECO

The Art Deco era represented the energy, modernity and innovation of the new century. Between 1920 and 1940 designers and architects broke away from the constraints of Victorian and Edwardian design to create a look that was dynamic yet simple, glamorous yet comfortable. The term Art Deco was, in fact, coined in the 1960s, and derived from the seminal design show of 1925, the Exposition Internationale des Arts Décoratifs et Industriels Modernes. Held in Paris, it was visited by 16 million people, who

Opposite, above and below: *The Art Deco style reigned supreme from the 1920s until until the outbreak of World War II. The living room shown in the top image is likely to have been that of an affluent family. But this style was not just for the elite. By the 1930s, mass production meant that everyone could live in the deco style, as the more middle-class room in the lower image shows. The stained-glass sunray windows so prevalent in the 1930s streets of Britain show that this really was a style for everyone.*

were presented with a vision of modernity in designs for architecture, furniture, fashion, and the decorative arts.

Art Deco style was bold and geometrical, with sweeping curves and strong, often abstract shapes and motifs such as sunbursts, chevrons, and fountains. It moved away from the romance of Art Nouveau and the homeliness of Arts and Crafts, to produce a look that reflected modern living – streamlined, sophisticated, and confident.

Interpretations of the Art Deco style became visible in newly built homes of the 1920s and 1930s, and public buildings such as Tube stations, offices, and cinemas; BBC Broadcasting House, the Dorchester Hotel, and the Hoover factory, all in London, are fine examples. Large windows filled rooms with light, and enhanced with white schemes accented by black and grey. New and luxurious materials, such as chrome, ebony, marble, sharkskin, and Bakelite – an early plastic – were incorporated into designs for furniture and appliances.

Big-name designers and makers of the time included René Lalique, who focused solely on glass during the Art Deco period; the sculptors Josef Lorenzl and Demêtre Chiparus, who made exquisite bronze figures in the shape of slim dancers; and the ceramic designers Clarice Cliff and Susie Cooper, whose colourful, quirky designs typify the uplifting spirit of Art Deco.

INSPIRATIONAL INTERIOR

The entrance hall at Eltham Palace is the last word in Art Deco elegance and glamour, a space made for sipping champagne. The house, which is adjacent to the late 15th-century Eltham Palace, in south-east London, was completed in 1936 for the Courtauld textiles heir, Stephen Courtauld, and his wife Virginia. The couple decked out their new home in luxurious and exotic materials ranging from blackbean and bird's eye maple wall veneers to gold leaf, onyx, and pink leather upholstery. Even their beloved pet lemur, Mah-Jongg, lived in a heated cage with wall murals.

This room contains many Art Deco elements, from the geometric rug and coffee tables, to the simple white leather chairs, and the rich wood panelling.

ART DECO ANTIQUES

With an obsession for new materials and techniques, Art Deco design epitomizes the "machine age" of the early 20th century. Many designs reflect an appreciation of the Neo-classical style – rectilinear and symmetrical case furniture, or urn- and baluster-shaped glass and ceramics, for example – and there is a return to forms that emerged during the Regency period (see p.150) with a similar emphasis on luxury. Richly figured bird's eye maple, walnut, and macassar ebony veneers contrast with minimal ivory or lacquerwork decoration in many pieces of furniture. Other designs embrace new materials like aluminium, chrome, and Bakelite, which are ideally suited to the "streamlined" or skyscraper items that reflect a fascination with progress and speed. The "suite" took root during this period – look out for bedroom furniture with a number of matching pieces, or three-piece living room suites of "cloud" furniture, so-called on account of the shapely sofa and chair backs.

Instead of looking back to ancient Greece and Rome for inspiration, as the Neo-classicists had done, Art Deco designers instead used geometric designs inspired by the Aztecs and ancient Egypt. Common motifs are stepped Aztec-like pyramid forms, stylized sunbursts, scarab beetles, and chevrons. Similar themes are evident in glassmaking, metalware, and ceramics, where traditional Classical shapes, such as the urn, are embellished with geometric patterns, step motifs, or stylized animal forms (notably stags and hounds). The female figure continues to be as important as for Art Nouveau designers but has undergone a significant change. Here, she is thoroughly modern, athletic and assertive, with short, almost masculine hair.

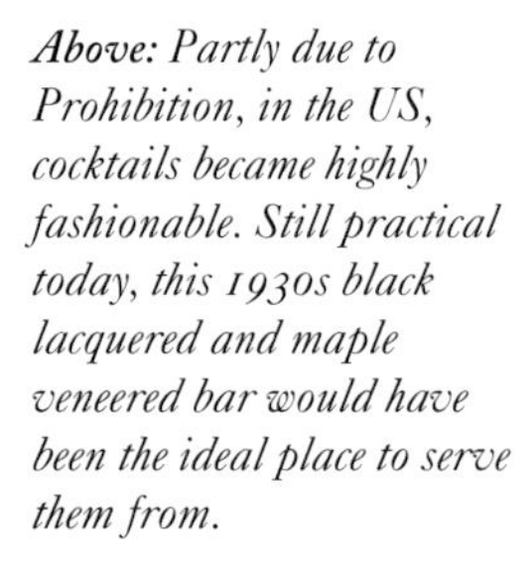

Above: *Partly due to Prohibition, in the US, cocktails became highly fashionable. Still practical today, this 1930s black lacquered and maple veneered bar would have been the ideal place to serve them from.*

Right: *Elegant animals such as dogs, leaping gazelles, and polar bears appear frequently in the Art Deco style. This graceful patinated bronze dog is in the style of Austrian sculptor Karl Hagenauer.*

Above: Luxurious woods and geometric lines are combined in these late 1920s beech and palisander armchairs.

DESIGN HERO

Born in Austria, Josef Lorenzl (1892–1950) was a prolific sculptor of, mostly, female figures in the Art Deco style. His designs were beautiful – tall, languid women in all manner of dancing poses, but almost always balancing on the toes of just one foot. Sometimes partially clothed, often naked, Lorenzl's women exude feminine elegance. Most of his statues were case in bronze that was then either silvered or gilded, while a number of them had hands and faces carved from ivory. Lorenzl's designs inspired thousands of copies, typically made in spelter, which are more affordable today.

An Austrian gilt metal figurine of a dancing lady, designed by Josef Lorenzl, and marked 'Lorenzl Made In Austria', on an onyx socle.

MODERNISM

Modernism was not one rigid movement, but rather an evolution of ideas over a number of decades that fuelled much of the design and architecture of the 20th century. In an age of progress and rapidly accelerating technology, Modernists felt a prevailing desire to create a better, healthier world through buildings and furnishings. They believed that they could transform society through design.

Prime movers in spreading this philosophy were the Bauhaus school of crafts

Opposite, above and below: Modernists believed that 'form follows function'. It is difficult for us to appreciate how radical the resulting idea of having no extra ornamentation in a room was. It was a total departure from the obsession with historical revivals that had dominated the centuries before. In the room shown at the top of the opposite page, Mies van der Rohe's Barcelona day bed (designed in 1930) perfectly epitomises the clean lines of this style. Yet the chairs shown are not by the same designer – avoid modern imitations of classic pieces if you can.

and fine arts in Weimar, Germany, founded in 1919 and closed by the Nazis in 1933. The school advocated that functionality of design should rule over form. The Swiss-born French architect Le Corbusier also challenged traditional ideas of architecture, using materials such as concrete and glass to create designs that were utilitarian yet nurturing.

Modernists made a break with the historic traditions of interior style by embracing the principles of simplicity, economy, and utility. The goal of teaming technical innovation with functionality fed into a wide range of designers' work from the 1920s onward. Among the most iconic is Marcel Breuer's "Wassily" chair, designed in 1925, which turned the concept of a gentleman's club chair on its head by using a tubular steel and leather construction, rather than wood and fabric.

Ludwig Mies van der Rohe designed his famous "Barcelona" chair in 1929, using stainless steel for the frame and panels of leather for the upholstery. Alvar Aalto's 1931–2 design for the plywood Paimio chair launched a thousand pretenders, while Eileen Gray's 1927 "E-1027" adjustable glass and metal side table has also earned a place in design history.

In London, modernist hotspots include Wells Coates's Isokon Flats in Lawn Road, Hampstead, with signature built-in furniture, and Ernö Goldfinger's 1937–9 home in Willow Road, Hampstead, complete with his own furniture designs.

The Villa Savoye contains many of Le Corbusier's most notable furniture designs, including the Gran Confort chair designed with Charlotte Perriand and Pierre Jeanneret in 1929, and the famous 8306 lounger designed with Perriand in 1928.

INSPIRATIONAL INTERIORS

Built in 1929–31 as a weekend retreat for the owners, the Villa Savoye at Poissy in France is Le Corbusier's most famous building. The architect described his villas as "machines for living in" and "machines for moving people emotionally". Stilts known as pilotis separate the living quarters from the damp earth, and a roof garden encourages outdoor living. The exterior of the house is painted white, but inside are blocks of colour amid the open-plan layout and panoramic windows.

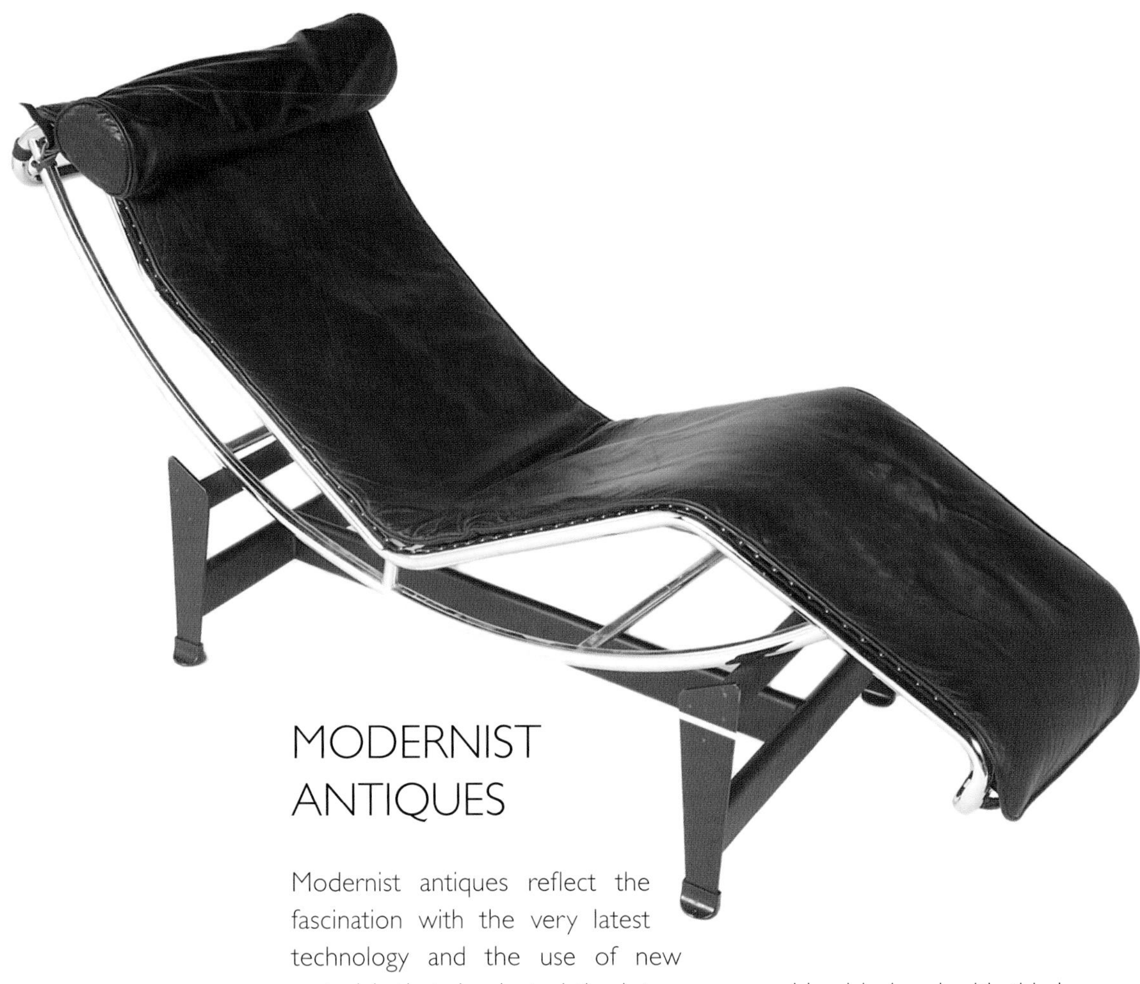

MODERNIST ANTIQUES

Modernist antiques reflect the fascination with the very latest technology and the use of new materials that dominated the interwar years. Hand in hand with this is an emphasis on paring back to the absolute minimum all items for the home – and the home itself. The function of a piece is paramount and all surface ornament is abandoned, with the exception of a few areas of flat colour here and there. The resulting look is clinical and industrial, echoing the ethos of the time.

Typical furniture is overwhelmingly geometric, made from bent plywood or chrome-plated bent tubular steel, with the structure of a piece being clearly visible. The upholstery of choice is leather, restricted to a very minimal palette – often black, but also white and tan – and glass features frequently for tabletops. Seminal pieces include the cantilever chair in various manifestations and the chaise longue (the latter far removed from opulent Regency or Victorian examples); the first stacking chairs date from this time.

In ceramics, motifs are minimal and often abstract. The influence of Japan is still present, alongside new themes inspired by the De Stijl, Constructivist, and Cubist movements. Studio pottery is simplified compared with pieces made during the Art Nouveau and Art Deco periods, yet dynamic and functional. Mass-produced glass reflects the ongoing obsession with clean, functional, decoration – metal pieces are now made from stainless steel and aluminium. Typical textiles involve repeating geometric and abstract patterns.

Above: *Beloved of loft-living urbanites, and an icon of Modernist furniture, the 8306 day bed designed by Le Corbusier and Charlotte Perriand in 1928 is as much a sculpture as a piece of furniture. Still available from Cassina today, it is made from chrome plated tubular steel, iron and leather upholstery. Avoid buying modern, unlicensed imitations, as the quality is usually much lower, and they do not represent good investments.*

Above: *Based on a 1939 design by Egon Riss, this painted wood Isokon 'Penguin Donkey' bookcase was designed by Ernest Race in 1963, and was originally produced to hold eighty of Penguin famous paperbacks.*

DESIGN HERO

The only woman working independently in her field at this time, Irish-born Eileen Gray (1878-1976) remained relatively obscure outside design circles for most of her life. In the late 1960s and early 1970s, however, she came to the attention of a wider public following an article about her work in Domus magazine and the revival of a few pieces by the London-based furniture company Aram. Gray's style was more opulent than that of her contemporaries, and although she is best remembered for her "Bibendum" chair and the "E-1027" side table – exemplary and influential pieces of the modernist age – she also designed exquisite lacquered blockwork screens more in keeping with the Art Deco style.

These adjustable chrome and glass E–1027 tables were designed c1928 to enable one of Gray's sisters to indulge her love of breakfast in bed.

MID CENTURY MODERN

World War II may have put design on hold for a decade, but by the 1950s there was no shortage of talent. Young designers were impatient to change the face of interiors once more, and the public yearned for homes that were fresh, optimistic, and filled with colour to counteract the drab greyness of post-war life.

The Festival of Britain in 1951 made a break with the past and launched the careers of designers such as Robin and Lucienne Day (designers of furniture

Opposite, above and below: The term Mid Century Modern was coined only in 1983 but it is now recognized by scholars and museums worldwide as a significant design movement. Scandinavian designers and architects were very influential at this time, with a style characterized by simplicity, democratic design and natural shapes. The Lounger armchair was designed in 1952 for S Hille & Co. by the renowned British designer Robin Day (b.1915), a year after he rose to prominence during the highly influential Festival of Britain.

and textiles respectively), Clive Latimer, and Ernest Race. The London store Heal's became a showcase, and companies such as Ercol and Hille in Britain and Knoll in the United States produced exciting furniture collections.

In contrast to the geometrical designs of Art Deco and modernism, the Mid-century Modern designers returned to organic shapes derived from nature. As well as working with wood they used materials such as polyurethane, fibreglass, and metal mesh. The clean lines of Scandinavian design were also a big influence. Chair design in particular underwent a revolution. Among the roll call of iconic seats are Eero Saarinen's 1956 "Tulip" chair in upholstered plastic; Harry Bertoia's 1952 "Diamond" chair made from a moulded mesh of chrome-plated steel wire; Charles and Ray Eames's seminal fibreglass "DAR" chair (standing for Dining Armchair Rod) of 1950, the first predominantly plastic chair to be mass-produced, and the first not to be upholstered; and Robin Day's 1950 "Hillestak" stacking chair with a plywood seat, curved plywood back, and beech legs.

Glassmaking was enjoying a renaissance too. The Swedish manufacturer Kosta epitomized the Scandinavian style, with its thick-walled vases in asymmetrical, curvy shapes decorated with delicate patterning. Glassblowers on the Venetian island of Murano put the emphasis on scintillating colour created with coloured canes and murrines displayed within contemporary shapes. In Britain the Whitefriars glass studio created its own bold, textured pieces, such as "Bark" and "Banjo".

INSPIRATIONAL INTERIOR

Although it was the first skyscraper in Copenhagen, the SAS Royal Hotel designed in 1960 by Arne Jacobsen (1902–71) is best known today for its interior design. Many of Jacobsen's most famous designs were produced for it, including the 'Egg' and 'Drop' chairs of 1958 (shown in Situ above), and the AJ pendant lamp. Even the curtains, cutlery and doorhandles were designed by Jacobsen. As such, it represents a superb example of a complete interior by a world–famous Mid-century Modern designer.

Room 606 is the only remaining room that has been left as Jacobsen intended. It gives a valuable insights into how colour and furniture were used.

MID-CENTURY MODERN ANTIQUES

With Scandinavia and the United States taking the lead, antiques most closely associated with the immediate post-war years are often described as 'soft modernism'. A form-follows-function ethos is still maintained, in which furniture remains rectilinear and geometric, with little surface decoration, but pieces are softer, warmer, easier on the eye, and more comfortable. There is an emphasis on small-scale pieces for the post-war domestic environment – clever compact storage and stacking furniture – as well as on greater comfort for day-to-day living.

Above left: The 'Homemaker' range of tableware designed in 1957 by Enid Seeney for Ridgway is one of the best known Mid-century Modern ranges of ceramics. It was originally sold inexpensively in Woolworth's.

Alongside the use of traditional woods, such as teak, rosewood, and walnut, experiments in steel and bent plywood continue with stunning results, and new materials include moulded fibreglass and polystyrene foam padding. Both are suitable for creating organic, curvaceous forms, the latter upholstered in single-colour stretch fabrics. Minimalism is expressed in the desire to create forms from the bare minimum, cheaply, and on a large scale. For example, a chair may be made from a single sheet of plywood or from fibreglass-reinforced plastic. Traditional cabinet-making methods are revived in tandem with mass-production technologies, and experiments in narrow-gauge steel lead to a number of innovative pieces. Seminal forms include the sideboard – a modern take on Neo-classical commodes and Regency side cabinets – the coffee table, and the lounge chair.

Developments in ceramics, glassmaking, silverware, and textiles reflect similar trends. Look for sculptural, organic forms, often in single colours. Ceramics may be decorated with subtle geometric patterns or domestic designs that reflect the growing demand for a wide range of homewares.

Left: Arne Jacobsen's 1957–58 'Swan' chair, named after the curves that echo those of a swan's profile, is made from moulded fibreglass, foam, and aluminium.

***Above:** The cool colours and curving, organic form of this 'Minuet' range vase are typical of 1950s Scandinavian glass design. It was designed for Holmegaard by Per Lütken.*

***Right:** This 1950s Venini fazzoletto, or 'handkerchief', vase was designed by Paolo Venini and Fulvio Bianconi c1949. Since then, the form has been copied by other factories both on the Italian island of Murano, and in other countries.*

DESIGN HEROES

The American husband and wife team of Charles (1907-78) and Ray (1912-88) Eames is synonymous with Mid-century Modern furniture design. Through innovative experimentation with the latest materials – plywood, fibreglass-reinforced plastics, and narrow-gauge steel – their stated aim was to get "the most of the best to the greatest number of people for the least amount of money". Their ingenuity lay in producing the basic shell of a piece – a plywood or fibreglass chair seat, for example – and then widening the choice to the public by giving that same piece steel legs, a pedestal base, or rockers, and then producing it in a range of colours. Revolutionary and highly influential, their status of design heroes is confirmed by the fact that many of their designs are still produced today.

The 670 Lounge Chair and ottoman of c1956 was based on the level of comfort a soft, well-worn baseball glove may offer.

1960s & 1970s

With the deprivations of World War II a memory, the home-owners of the 1960s embraced modern style with a vengeance, and new design started to filter down into ordinary homes. For example, the Danish designer Arne Jacobsen had created his classic "Egg", "Swan", and "Ant" chairs in the late 1950s, but the desirability of his organic designs only increased in the 1960s.

Experimentation was in the air, from the exploration of space – the first moon

Opposite, above and below: *The influence of pop art and op art can be seen clearly in the design of the 1960s and 1970s. The shapes are adventurous and experimental, with modern synthetic materials contorted into all manner of shapes at the whim of the designer. Space-age influence was everywhere, from the design of television sets that look like an astronaut's helmet to the futuristic dining table and chairs in the kitchen shown opposite. The chair in the living room shown below it is the influential Elda Chair (see p. 181), which was designed by Joe Colombo c1964.*

landing was in 1969 – to the craze of Beatlemania and the hippy Summer of Love in 1967. Bridget Riley's Op Art paintings of black and white geometrical patterns summed up the futuristic feel.

In line with social influences, designers created pod-shaped furniture in leather, plastic, bamboo, and wicker. Jazzy, colourful wallpaper and posters covered walls. And teak was a popular wood for furniture, used in its solid form or as veneer on slimline styles for smaller homes.

Designers drew on the past for inspiration. The beautiful whiplash curves of Art Nouveau were transformed into psychedelia, and Victoriana became popular again – think stripped pine furniture, vintage stone bottles foraged from the dump, and jet jewellery. In 1964 Terence Conran opened his first Habitat store in Chelsea, with the aim of making good design available to everyone. His array of lifestyle products chimed well with the trend for open-plan living, home entertaining, and the increasingly informal ways in which families relaxed at home in front of the TV.

In the 1970s the theme of comfort grew apace. A decorating palette of nature-inspired greens, velvety browns, oranges, and oatmeal was used on everything from walls and upholstery to soft furnishings and bathroom suites. Furniture moved on from the slender Scandinavian look to a more chunky appearance, with well-upholstered sofas and reclining chairs. This was the second age of pine, too – cheap and versatile.

INSPIRATIONAL INTERIOR

On the Côte d'Azur near Théoule-sur-Mer is an architectural wonder of the late 20th century. Le Palais Bulles, or Palace of Bubbles, built into the cliff face, is a breathtaking cascade of spherical rooms in the colour of the surrounding rock. A typical 1960–70s vision of the future, it is the home of the fashion designer and collector Pierre Cardin and was designed by the architect Antti Lovag. Straight out of the space age, it also echoes the cave dwellings of thousands of years ago.

The ceiling aperture, painted spheres on the walls, and the furniture echo not only the space–aged theme, but also the overall form of the house.

1960s & 1970s ANTIQUES

Many antiques dating from this period reflect a surge in the experimentation with new forms – thanks, in part, to the plastics revolution that took place in the 1960s but also to the rise of popular culture that permeated all aspects of day-to-day living. In terms of furniture, there was an emphasis on fun, sculptural forms that made maximum use of not only the malleability of these new plastics, but also their low manufacturing costs, and appealed specifically to the young generation. Huge swivel armchairs and multi-part sectional storage systems on wheels were typical. Innovations in injection moulding revolutionized chair design in particular, leading to the creation of single-piece designs moulded entirely from plastic or fibreglass. Seminal furniture designs from this period include space-age balls and bubbles for lounging in and the world's first plastic cantilevered chairs. The same innovations in technology paved the way for all manner of disposable homewares, from dining services to electronic goods.

Toward the end of this period, pieces begin to reflect the "anti-design" sentiment that dominated the last decades of the 20th century. By now, the strong linear and geometric designs of modernist and Mid-century Modern forms are gone; there is less interest in "good form" and a new-found respect for asymmetry. Designs became loaded with irreverence. Expect to see pieces that challenge precepts of good taste – such as furniture laminated in garish plastics – and forms that either appropriate older styles or incorporate objets trouvés into their designs.

The emphasis on bright colours, historical motifs and often asymmetrical designs characterize the glassware and ceramics produced during this period, too.

***Above:** The 1970s Panasonic 'Toot–a–loop' radio could be positioned on a table, or worn as a bangle on a wrist when swivelled closed. It was available in a range of coloured plastics. Lime green is rare.*

***Left:** The vivid colours and stylised leaf and flower motifs on this charger from Poole's 'Delphis' range typify the 1960s & 1970s.*

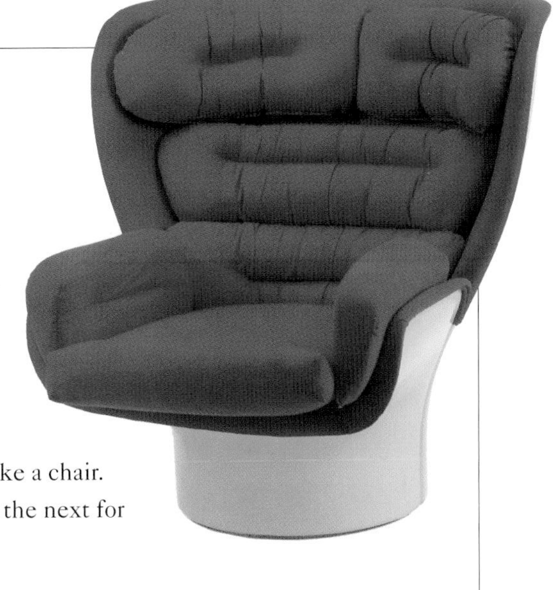

DESIGN HERO

Joe Colombo (1930–71) exhibited an incredible affinity with the materials at his disposal and was tireless in his pursuit of new forms. An unrivalled sense of practicality underpins many of his ground-breaking designs. In his "Elda" chair he created a huge fibreglass shell with leather cushions that cocooned the sitter, but could also be removed for cleaning. His "Tube" consisted of four comfy tubes that could be assembled in any order to make a chair. The tubes were different sizes so that each fitted inside the next for compact storage.

Designed c1964, and named after his wife, Colombo's swivelling 'Elda' chair was technically advanced in its use of fibreglass.

***Below:** Reminiscent of an astronaut's helmet, the futuristic 'Dalu' lamps designed c1968 by the Italian Vico Magistretti for Artemide, are made of a single piece of moulded plastic. Transparent versions are modern re–editions.*

ECLECTIC

At the beginning of the 21st century we have so many gorgeous styles to choose from that it can be hard to know where to start when buying furniture or creating an interior scheme. The fashion for matching styles of furnishing to each other has given way to a style known as Eclectic, where all kinds of period styles and pieces can be drawn together to create a very individual look. In fact, this style is not so new and in essence can be seen in the traditional style of Britain's country houses. These grand homes,

Opposite, top: Styles from different periods work to great visual effect in this pared down Georgian panelled room. The sofa is in the 18th century rococo style, the polyurethane 'Up 1' chair was designed by Gaetano Pesce in 1969, and the lamp is contemporary.

Opposite, bottom left: Continental gilt brass candleholders with opalescent glass flowers from a church accentuate the Rococo lines of the early 20th century carved French bed, giving an eclectic, 21st century vibe when combined with a vividly coloured wall.

sometimes open to the public, often display objects and furnishings that have been collected and added to over the centuries and meld seamlessly together. Chatsworth in Derbyshire is a fine example, where 16 generations of one family have acquired a fabulous collection of antique and contemporary furniture, paintings, and sculpture that look breathtaking displayed together.

The Eclectic style is not a hotchpotch, but needs a little thought and planning. Pieces from different eras tend to work better against a neutral decorating scheme that acts as a unifying canvas – shades such as grey, taupe, or off-white are preferred. Stronger decorating colours can work, too, as long as they are closely related to each other in the colour spectrum: a plummy paint shade, for example, with a feature wallpaper in a similar hue.

Lovers of the Eclectic style often have one or two statement pieces that act as focal points in the room. They also take into consideration the relationship between shape and proportion. This allows furnishings as diverse as an organic-shaped 1960s chair and a curvy Georgian sofa, or a slim Danish Mid-century Modern side table and a slender Regency console, to sit well together, because the lines reflect each other.

INSPIRATIONAL INTERIOR

"Baroque courtesan's parlour meets Parisian antiques market" is how Hassan Abdullah, Michel Lassere, and Stefan Karlson describe the fantastical interiors of their restaurant, Les Trois Garçons, in London's Whitechapel area. Diners are overlooked by stuffed animals, sit beneath sparkling chandeliers, and are surrounded by grand antiques. The building was originally an old pub that the trio, antiques dealers and designers, first converted into a private residence and then a restaurant in 2000. Les Trois Garçons is a masterclass in Eclectic style, courageously and shamelessly blending pieces from different eras without a hiccup.

A 1950s Serge Mouille chandelier, a 1960s Perspex bubble chair, and contemporary art vie for attention in the colourful Annex of the private apartment of Les Trois Garçons.

ECLECTIC ANTIQUES

If you have a passion for more than one of the styles described in this chapter, you might seek a more eclectic look for your home, buying pieces from a number of different eras. This is not akin to the high Victorian period, which was awash with various revival-style reproductions and pastiches, but involves a carefully considered approach to creating a homogenous look. There is an emphasis on uniting pieces from different eras by colour, texture, form, scale, or some other common theme. Neutral colours are key for walls, floors, and large-scale pieces, where too many diverse designs could tip the balance in the wrong direction.

A number of apparently diverse period styles can work well together because they share themes – the sinuous forms of the French Rococo and Art Nouveau periods, for example, or the more symmetrical forms of the Regency and Art Deco periods. Or there might be a focus on just one furniture form throughout the house – say, chairs – where the most influential pieces of each stylistic period feature in different rooms. Another approach would be to collect only rare and limited edition pieces, or items that do not necessarily conform to the defining style of the period in which they were made, or pieces that are extreme interpretations of a given style. There are no hard and fast rules.

Above: *Reminiscent of orbiting planets, satellites or astronaut's helmets, this 1960s chrome table lamp would add a futuristic feel to any interior and, because of its curves, would work well alongside the rocker below.*

Right: *The modern look of this polished iron and black leather rocking chair by R. W. Winfield & Co. belie its origins in the 1850s. Bold, eccentric, and visually appealing pieces such as these are highly sought–after today.*

Far left: Italian designer Gaetano Pesce's idiosyncratic designs make him popular amongst those building an eclectic look. His 1986 stiffened felt and polyester padded 'Feltri' chair is typical of his work.

Left: Postmodern designer and architect Ettore Sottsass was inspired by the neon lights of cities like Las Vegas when designing this 'Asteroid' table lamp for Poltronova in 1968.

DESIGN HERO

The Italian designer Piero Fornasetti (1913–88) has a staggering 11,000 designs to his name, ranging from ceramics and textiles to furniture. Despite criticism and derision from his Modernist and Mid-century Modern peers, he persevered in expressing his very personal, often surreal style. Trained in the fine arts, Fornasetti loved to experiment with Classical three-dimensional decoration on a two-dimensional plane. Among his many successes are the complex architectural scenes that he screen-printed onto laminated surfaces (inside and out) of a range of furniture pieces designed by his contemporary, Gio Ponti. Today, his eccentric designs are incredibly popular.

Designed by Fornasetti in 1987, the minimal form of this 'Pompeian' corner cabinet displays his hallmark architectural surface design perfectly.

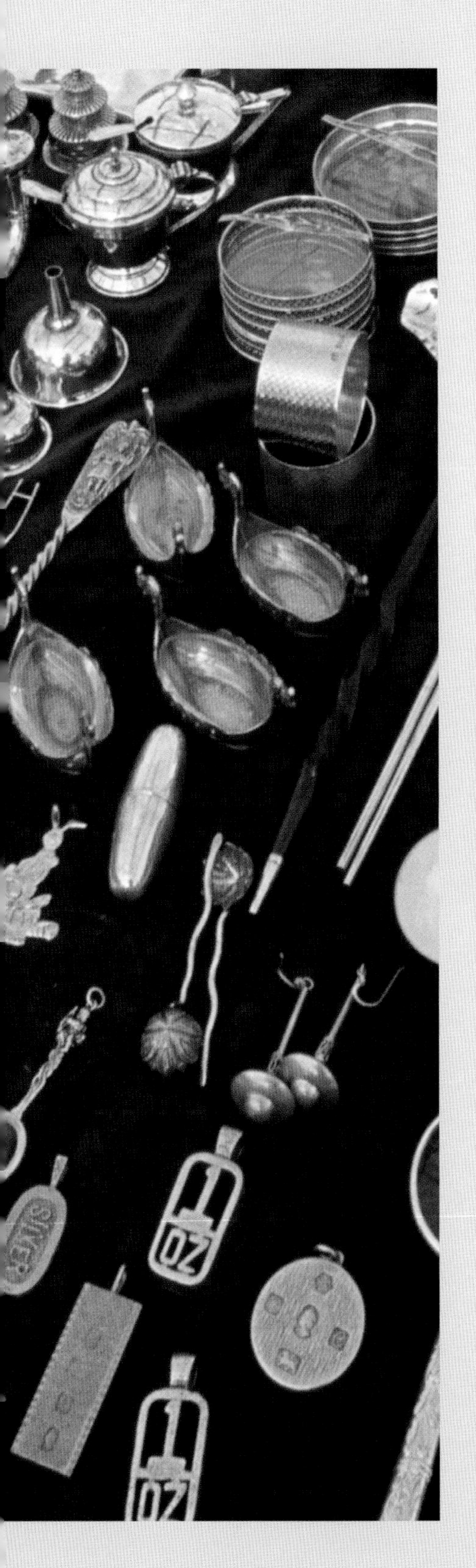

RESOURCES

BUYING AT A FAIR OR FROM DEALERS

Previous pages: *An array of silver and silver plated jewellery and other items strikingly displayed for sale at a regional antiques fair.*

Opposite: *20th century ceramics by renowned makers and designers, including Clarice Cliff, Susie Cooper, Moorcroft. Royal Worcester, Troika and Crown Derby, are for sale on this stand at a major antiques fair.*

Some of the most exciting events in the antiques calendar are the big fairs that occur throughout the year where, depending on size and location, thousands of dealers stall up, come rain or shine, to sell their wares. Here you get the chance to browse at leisure in the open air, to pick out anything that takes your fancy. You will find everything from large-scale pieces of furniture to Art Deco silverware, and from Whitefriars glass to vintage fabrics. The choice is endless and suitable for all tastes and pockets.

By far the biggest of these fairs is held at Newark in Nottinghamshire. Reputedly the largest antiques fair in Europe, it boasts some 4,000 stalls. The Arthur Swallow fair at Lincolnshire Showground, near Lincoln, often has 3,000 stalls. These two fairs often occur in the same week, so you might need to decide which is best for you. The biggest fair in the south of England is held at Ardingly in West Sussex, with 1,700 stalls. All three fairs are held six times a year and attract sellers (and buyers) from all over Europe, including dealers from France, Belgium, Germany, and the Netherlands.

Smaller fairs are held across the country – run by the IACF (International Antiques and Collectors Fairs, who also run the Newark and Ardingly fairs). Some of the better-known fairs are held at Shepton Mallet in Somerset, Detling in Kent, and Swinderby in Lincolnshire.

WHAT TO EXPECT AT A FAIR

Larger fairs, such as those listed on the preceding page, are run over two or three days, with the first day reserved for trade buyers and the remainder open to the public at large, which is when you can go. Parking is free, but you should expect to pay an entrance fee. You can find more information about the fairs on the relevant websites (see p.213).

At each fair, the majority of stalls are lined up in avenues big enough to drive down (allowing buyers to collect their goods at the end of the day) and almost as far as the eye can see. It may appear chaotic, but regular dealers usually stall out in the same spot at every fair, making it easy for you to make a beeline for them. There are also stalls in marquees. These tend to contain furniture and the more valuable antiques, although this is not always the case, so don't dismiss them. Top-end silver, jewellery, ceramics, and collectables can usually be found in the more permanent building in the grounds.

Below: A 1930s celluloid Kewpie doll, a 1970s Thomas Dam troll and a Disney Goofy figurine sit amidst this collection of toys, evoking a strong sense of nostalgia.

The procedure is pretty much the same whichever fair you go to. As a buyer, you wander up and down the avenues, stopping to take a closer look at something that takes your fancy. Examine it carefully, and ask any questions you might like to. In most cases, items are not priced in any way, so you have to ask the seller. You will hear other buyers asking, "What's the best on...?" or "What can you do on...?" All sellers expect to offer some kind of discount at a fair – it is routine. Depending on what you are looking at, and how you feel about its price and condition, you could haggle a little before committing. Always be polite and try to gauge the mood of the seller, though. If they say, "There's no more room in it" or "That's my best", pushing any further might sour the deal. Purchases at antiques fairs are always made in cash – there are few chip-and-pin machines here – but many dealers are reluctant to take cheques from any but their most regular customers.

If you have never been to an antiques fair and are serious about buying vintage and antique furniture and ornaments for your home, you simply cannot leave it any longer. It really is a thrill to see so many things in one spot, and the dealer camaraderie is unrivalled. This is also one of the few occasions on

Above: *Antiques and collectors' fairs are true treasure troves, where you can find anything from Victorian-style magnifying glasses to Royal commemorative ceramics, photographs of rock and pop stars, to vintage glassware, all for everything from a couple of pounds upwards.*

which you can browse at leisure without feeling the inhibition you might feel in a small antiques shop, the pressure you might feel at an auction, or that sense of sterile purchase that can accompany buying online. Due to prevailing fashions, prices for much run-of-the-mill Georgian to Edwardian furniture are also at a low point, even though the market is showing signs of recovery. There really has never been a better time to buy.

But don't get too carried away with the ease of it all! Plan your trip wisely. First, consider the weather. All of these fairs are outdoor events, and many of them take the best part of the day to visit. Picture a muddy field in the driving rain, all the stalls sheeted over with plastic to protect the wares but making it impossible to spot the bargains, and it might not seem such a glamorous proposition. The same can be said for a hot summer's day, where you will find no shelter from the sun. A good time to go for a first visit, therefore, might be a spring or autumn fair, which will be busy in dealer terms and where the

Right: *Vintage Bakelite telephones like this 1930s-50s G.P.O. 300 series model, can be rewired for use today. Red and green are rare and more valuable than black. Modern reproductions or copies are usually lighter in weight, made from a different plastic, and bear flatter moulded numbers on the handset.*

weather might not be so punishing. Even then, it is a good idea to take adequate protection, whether this is a coat or suncream, and, above all, to wear sensible shoes.

If you have a number of things on your wish list, or expect to be making regular visits to fairs, you might also want to get hold of a trolley, which will save you making return trips to the car. You can bring your car into the fair to collect, in which case write down every purchase and a note of where you bought it. It is all to easy to leave the fair with something missing. Even the most experienced dealers have been known to forget purchases.

WHAT TO EXPECT AT ANTIQUES SHOPS

Below: *Building up a group of different antique cups and saucers is more fun, and often more affordable, than buying a new set from the high street.*

Many dealers who attend the fairs also have shops in cities and towns throughout Britain, whether independent boutiques in an arcade, or as part of an antiques emporium, or even as an independent outlet. Whatever their circumstances, this is by far the most personal way of buying antiques. Invariably you are dealing with someone who has great enthusiasm for their stock, and who is therefore more knowledgeable about the pieces on display. Make friends with a dealer. Over time, they may be willing to look out for certain pieces or to suggest contacts where you might find them. As well as offering invaluable advice, after time (and purchases) you may also qualify for a better discount.

Dealers tend to fall into two categories: those who sell anything that they like (a mix of furniture, lighting, ceramics, and glass regardless of period) and those who specialize by period, or look, or type of antique. This usually means that, in any town, you have a wide range of dealers to choose from and may find a number of them useful for different reasons. It is always a delight to step into an antiques shop, as goods are usually arranged beautifully in order to show them off to best effect. Unlike at the outdoor fairs, the dealer has time to display their wares with more care and space.

Also unlike the fairs, most dealers have clearly visible price tags on their wares. This does not mean that the prices are not negotiable, however – you can still expect to get some kind of discount if you ask, though it may not be as generous as those at the fairs. There are several reasons for this. The fairs generate a selling mood, with dealers really enjoying shifting a good number of pieces, while shops have less pressure to sell in such a short time. In addition, since buying a piece, the dealer may have had to spend more money on it – say, a little restoration, or a second purchase to make a set – and each time they spend money, any profit on the piece is diminished. They are therefore unlikely to want to discount the piece by very much. However, there are also circumstances in which the dealer may look favourably on a discount. Perhaps the piece came as a larger group at a good price, or it has been in the shop for a while and the dealer is keen to sell. Be polite, but it never hurts to ask.

Below: Pieces that are typical of a particular style, or of the period they were made in, usually make excellent buys. Every element of this 1930s French Bakelite clock by Blangy illustrates the Art Deco style.

NO HIDDEN EXTRAS

One of the great advantages of buying at a fair or from a dealer is that the price you agree is always the final price, while other buying options carry hidden costs. At auctions you are obliged to pay a buyer's premium on any successful bid.. Online purchases often include the added cost of having the goods shipped to you.

BUYING AT AUCTION

Opposite: *A great auctioneer will keep the pace of an auction swift and smooth, and will control the bidding in a friendly, approachable manner. If an auctioneer is unsure of your intentions or actions, he or she will usually ask if you were intending to bid. Do not worry about having to remortgage your home to pay for an accidentally acquired Picasso!*

Nothing quite beats the thrill of buying vintage furniture and antiques at auction. In the first place, you are surrounded by all manner of intriguing items, ranging from furniture through ceramics, glassware, and silver to fine art. Once an auction starts, it is difficult not to get swept up in the excitement as each lot is swiftly despatched, the bids rising rapidly as buyers try to secure a deal, and the gavel finally coming down with the highest bid. Surely this has to be one of the most novel and exciting ways to furnish a home.

Buying at auction has several advantages over buying online and from antiques fairs. Primarily, you are allowed to view the lots before the sale day, which means you can handle them and examine them in your own time – a real advantage over online shopping – and without the pressure of other buyers getting in first, which can happen at a fair. You also have the benefit of bidding for an item alongside a host of dealers and other private buyers, whereas most antiques fairs are open to trade buyers the day before the public are allowed in, which means you do not always get the chance to see the best pieces on sale.

There are numerous auction houses across the country, ranging from the hugely prestigious Sotheby's and Christie's to countrywide groups such as Dreweatts to small, local-run provincial establishments. The frequency of sales varies from venue to venue, but most will have a general sale at least once a month. While some of the bigger auction houses have specialized sales – Important Early European Furniture or Japanese Art and Design, for example – most auctions include a wide range of goods including furniture, ceramics, glassware, silverware, lighting, toys, and paintings. There is, therefore, plenty of scope for picking up one or more items with which to furnish your home at any one sale. Most auction houses have informative websites with all the relevant information on upcoming sales – dates, times, and catalogue listings.

Below: The veneer, colour and decorative details (such as the handles) on this 18th century chest–on–chest match, showing the two pieces are original partners. Read the auction house's catalogue description carefully, look at the photograph, and ideally visit the auction view to ensure that any piece you are interested in is similarly original.

ADVANCE PREPARATION

All auction houses operate along similar lines. Several days before a sale, the auction house holds a viewing day, open to everyone with an interest. This gives potential buyers the chance to take a look at all of the lots available, at their leisure, and without the risk of something selling before they have finished. Armed with a catalogue (which you buy from the auction house) or by viewing lots online, you can look up the lot number of pieces that you are interested in to find out more about the item in question. In most cases this will include a general description of the piece, plus an idea of when it dates from. Obvious damage or restoration should be noted and there might even be details of the item's provenance, if known. Finally, there will always be a guide price, or estimate, as to the approximate value of the piece at auction in the current marketplace.

If you are interested in a piece, this is your one opportunity to handle it and to examine it in detail. Take note of any damage or similar that is not mentioned in the catalogue. Read the description again, to make sure you have noted all of the points, and pay particular attention to anything that says "as found" or "AF", as this might suggest something is not quite right. The attribution, description and estimates in the catalogue are the opinion of the auctioneers and may not always tally with your own ideas or expectations. You should therefore use this unique opportunity to discuss anything further with the auctioneer or a resident expert should you want to. You can also request a full "condition report" – a detailed examination by an expert.

Once satisfied that you have seen all that you need to of the lots you are interested in, you can carry out a little more research at home to find out more about them. This might involve taking a look at past catalogues (often available online) or price guide books to see how similar items have been described before, what their estimates were, and, crucially, what they sold for. Although you cannot expect the exact same thing to happen again, it is good to have a rough idea of likely prices as a guideline, particularly if you are new to buying antiques and have yet to get a feel for this.

WHAT TO EXPECT ON THE DAY

When sale day arrives, it can be a good idea to arrive early to see the start of the sale in progress and get some idea as to how it works. Sales can move at quite a pace and it helps to familiarize yourself with the action and to assess how the auctioneer increases his bids. Once you are visiting regularly, particularly for big sales with a large number of lots, you can try to time your arrival for several lots before your own so that you are not hanging around for too long. You are also not obliged to stay until the end of the auction, if all the pieces you were interested in have already been and gone.

On arrival you need to register with the auction house, and you will receive a

Below: At the auction view, a ticket bearing the lot and auction numbers will be attached to each item. Smaller items, like these portrait miniatures, will be contained in cabinets, accessed by a member of the auction house's staff.

Above: When bidding at auction for furniture, or other large items, factor in the logistics and costs of getting it, or them, back to your home. If you cannot do this yourself, auction houses will usually be able to recommend a shipper you can use.

bidding card or number. The protocol for bidding is the same wherever you go. The auctioneer typically starts the bidding a little below the estimate; if he has no takers, he starts lower, until someone bites. To enter the bidding on an item, which you can do at any time, you should raise your bidding card or number for the auctioneer to see clearly. Thereafter he or she will return to you to register your interest and you can either nod to increase the bid or shake your head to drop out of the bidding. The auctioneer will usually call out the next, higher bid amount which is usually in increments of £5 or £10, £50 or £100, and so on (depending on the value of the item in question.), although you may announce the amount of money you wish to bid each time.

Two things are paramount. First, you must have a very firm idea of how much you are willing to pay for an item and then stick to this. It is all too easy to get swept away in the heat of the moment, only to find you have committed to more than you wanted. Second, make sure that all of your bids are very clear. It's a good idea to look purposefully and directly at the auctioneer when

Below: If you chose to bid without attending the auction (see below), always aim to view the item before the auction to make sure you are happy with the description of the item, and its condition.
The desirability and value of a piece, like the 19th century Meissen urn below, will be dramatically reduced if it is damaged, so you would ideally check all the complex decoration for damage or restoration.

bidding, and look away after shaking your head when you finish. Leave nonchalant bidding to the professionals, or until you have more experience. The auctioneer's decision is final as to who won the bid, and you could come unstuck if there is any ambiguity on your part. If at the end of the bidding the price has not met the reserve – that is, the lowest value the seller wishes to achieve (see Should I Sell?, p.206) – the sale does not go through. The auctioneer will make whether you have won or lost a lot clear.

If you do manage to secure a sale, once the auctioneer writes your name or paddle number down next to the lot on his or her list, you are legally obliged to buy the item at the hammer price. You will also have to pay a buyer's premium (the auction house's cut), which is usually in the region of 15–20 percent, as well as VAT on the buyer's premium. Look for symbols next to the lot description, which may refer to additional taxes to be paid, such as VAT on the hammer price. If you cannot take the item immediately, you will have a few days in which to arrange collection. After that you may be charged a fee by the auctioneer for storing the piece.

BIDDING WITHOUT ATTENDING ON THE DAY

It is worth noting that you do not have to attend the auction house to bid for a piece in a live auction – there are several alternatives. First, on liking a piece at a pre-sale visit, you can leave an "absentee bid" with the auction house. If the highest bid on the day is lower than your bid, the piece is yours. You pay only the price of the last bid, plus the relevant increment, and not necessarily the full amount of your bid. For example, if you left a bid of £600 on a desk and the highest bid at the auction is £450, you would pay £450 plus the next increment (say, £25), so £475 (plus buyer's premium and VAT on that premium). You can also take part in the live auction on the phone, through a representative at the auction house, or online (see p.200). In fact, you can even view the items and the catalogue online at most auction houses, although it is still best, if the item is valuable enough, to see and handle the piece yourself before committing to purchase.

Finally, do not forget that there are sellers as well as buyers at auctions. Therefore, while bidding for the pieces in a sale, you might also choose to sell some of your own antiques at auction.

CLIENT CARD

BUYING ONLINE

Opposite: It is now more than possible to build your collection from the comfort of your own living room. Just make sure that you don't miss out on the fun of an auction or a fair.

Almost all of the many auction houses across the country have online facilities for viewing forthcoming auctions, downloading catalogues, and even bidding for items in a sale. This can be done either by leaving an online bid on the appropriate page of the auction website – in much the same way that you would leave an absentee bid in person (see p.199) – or by joining the live action via a direct online feed from the saleroom. As one auction house puts it, you can bid from "the comfort of your own home/office/beach"! You need to register with the auction house in advance, however, and you might be charged an additional fee for the privilege (over and above the buyer's premium). This could be a good way to buy antiques if you do not have the time or are unable to travel the distance to attend the live auction in person.

BUYING ON EBAY

You can also buy antiques (and many other things) from online auction websites, such as eBay, the huge international online auction and shopping site for both individuals and businesses. Its origins date back to 1995, when it was founded in the United States and which some reports claim has as many as 10 million users a day. Here, sellers post their wares up for auction, complete with descriptions of the goods. In many cases they include photographs to show what the pieces look like and the condition they are in. As a buyer on eBay, the most conventional procedure is to bid for an item, much as you would do in a real auction.

Below: Look out for badly or incorrectly described items in online auctions. Often attributed to glassworks on Murano, this vase is actually Czechoslovakian. Demand for, and values of, postwar Czech glass are rising fast, and this 'Rhapsody' range vase, designed in 1960 for the Mstisov glassworks by Frantisek Zemek, is an excellent example.

A deadline is set and you can leave bids at any time before the sale comes up. This could be a matter of days, weeks, or even months. As potential buyers leave their bids, the price rises in increments (say 25p, £1, £5, or £50), depending on the value of the piece. Sales operate on a "proxy bid" system, similar to that of leaving an absentee bid at an auction house. This means that, right from the beginning, you can place a maximum bid on a piece, in secret. As the auction takes place, the auction software places bids on your behalf, rising in the standard increments for the value of the piece, until your maximum bid is reached.

For example, you could place a bid of £10 on something that starts at £3. A second bidder, unaware of the level of your bid, may leave a bid of £5. Automatically, the bid will raise to £5.25, say, in your name. The second bidder may raise to £5.50, and the bid will raise to £5.75, again in your name. Having reached, say, £6.25 the second bidder may drop out, with you winning the bid and paying a total of £6.50 (the second bidder's last bid, plus the increment) and not the £10 maximum. Leaving a maximum bid in this way can often secure the item for you, as your maximum is unknown and may never be reached.

Other ways of buying on eBay include "buy it now" and "make me an offer". In the former, buyers have the opportunity to agree to buy the item at a price set in advance by the seller. This eliminates the need to enter into an auction. With "Make me an Offer", buyers have the chance to suggest a price to the seller, to which he or she may or may not agree. A negotiation could start from here, again eliminating the need to go to auction. These systems are applied at the discretion (and expense) of the seller.

ADVANTAGES OF BUYING ANTIQUES ONLINE

There are, without doubt, many advantages to buying antiques online. To begin with, the world is your oyster. You can source antiques in many countries across the globe, pay for them, and have them shipped to your home without ever having to leave the house. Of course, you are unlikely to ship, say, a large cabinet from India many times in your life, if at all, but there is no harm in looking to see the phenomenal resources available at your fingertips. And it is not as far-fetched as it sounds.

You can use auction house websites in different countries to see how their descriptions vary, what kind of estimates they are given, and how much they sell for. You can visit all manner of dealer websites in the same way, to find out what they specialize in, how they describe their goods, and how much they price them at. All this can play an important part in learning about the particular areas of interest to you, and getting a feel for how and where to buy.

For example, you might find prices of French Art Deco wares much more competitive on French dealers' websites than on English ones, simply because the French have access to so many more of them. You may also find that it does not cost very much more to ship an item from France than it does from somewhere in the UK.

The biggest advantage of surfing the Internet is that there really are no limits as to what is available to you online. Not only that, but you can use all manner of search engines to source even the rarest items at an incomprehensible speed. Furthermore, you do not have to travel far and wide to visit auctions, either to preview items or to bid on them in a sale.

Below: Just like flea markets and car boot sales, online auctions can be the ideal place to find inexpensive pieces that are not of sufficient value to be handled by auction houses or dealers. This 1950s–60s Italian small jug is typical.

PRECAUTIONS TO TAKE

There are, of course, disadvantages of buying from the Internet. The most obvious one is that you cannot always examine goods before buying them. This is such an important part of buying antiques – or anything for that matter – that it should not be underestimated. Quite often it is through the close examination of a piece that you get a feel for it, see for yourself any imperfections, and can assess whether or not it is genuine. Although most Internet resources have images of the pieces for sale – under no circumstances should you ever buy anything totally blind – they do not satisfy the same role. This is fine if you know what you are looking at. Before buying anything on the Internet, it is more imperative than when buying from fairs or auction houses that you have carried out enough background research using reliable reference materials such as guide books to convince you of your purchase.

Below: This 1970s Belgian leather pedestal armchair is made even more inviting by adding a sheepskin and extra cushion. The pattern on the cushion, and the sheepskin itself, are also in keeping with the style of the period.

A second issue when buying from the Internet is the credibility of the seller. With auction houses and most dealers, this should not be an issue. They may have been in the business for many years, even generations, and will have some kind of track record to which you can refer. At the very least, they may belong to an association, like the British Antique Dealers' Association (BADA), through which you can check them out. With organizations like eBay, it is not so much the credibility of the seller that you might question, but rather that of their knowledge. Not all sellers are experts in their field, and they may come across their wares through house clearances, boot sales, or some other means not requiring specialization. In offering descriptions of their goods, they may therefore know less than you, or might be tempted to copy information from descriptions of similar items on sale.

This means that you must always carefully check the information given about a piece. Buyers on eBay can benefit from the ratings that each seller is awarded, based on feedback from previous sales. You are able to ask sellers direct questions about pieces, and you should make the most of this facility if you are ever in any doubt. You are also at liberty to request additional photographs or to ask detailed questions about items if you feel a view is missing or in any way unclear. Sellers, be they private individuals or auction house staff will want to help as they will always be keen to sell the item in question. Of course, this aspect can be turned around – in some instances you could benefit from knowing more than the seller.

SHIPPING AND PAYMENT

Another issue when buying online is the cost of shipping. At an antiques fair or an auction, the price you pay is invariably the final price, and you take the goods home with you in your car or van. Online, any shipping costs are over and above what you pay for a piece, and this can vary. Depending on the piece in question, considerable packaging costs could also be involved. Although these are usually clearly stated wherever you are buying from, always carefully check the conditions for posting/shipping before you enter into an agreement. Finally, find out what your payment options are, and always choose the most secure method. Sellers on eBay are recommended to take payment via a secure payment system by credit or debit card, although some accept cheques if the funds are cleared before goods are shipped. Also, eBay has its own subsidiary business, PayPal, through which you can transfer money from your bank or by using a credit/debit card. This payment system is not exclusive to eBay and can be used for many online transactions.

Above: *Although light in weight, this mounted and gilded stag's head would require a large box and plenty of packaging materials to prevent it being damaged in transit.*

Right: *Smaller, more compact items of furniture, like this 1950s Continental magazine rack, can be packaged up and sent through parcel post, rather than requiring the services of a specialist shipper.*

SHOULD I SELL?

***Opposite:** It's always a good idea to know exactly what you have before selling it, especially at a car boot sale. Consult reference books to make sure that your trash isn't treasure.*

Over time, if you are buying antiques or vintage pieces for your home on a regular basis, you may come to a point at which you want to sell something. There may be several reasons for this. For example, you may move home and see this as a great opportunity for starting afresh. Or maybe the pieces you have no longer work with subsequent purchases in terms of size or style. Perhaps you have an eclectic range of things and want to narrow your style down to one or two favourite themes. It could also be that you have simply outgrown certain items and no longer feel so attached to them. Whatever your circumstances, this could be a good time to assess what you have and how you wish to move it on.

There are various ways in which you can do this, essentially using the same avenues that you use to buy – auction houses, antique dealers, trade fairs, and the Internet, each with its advantages and disadvantages.

And it is very useful to remember that, unlike buying flat-pack furniture, there is always the chance that any antique you buy will increase in value rather than diminish as it gets older.

SELLING AT AUCTION

This is the most popular method among private sellers. There is invariably an auction house in the nearest reasonably sized town, and the procedure is easy to follow. In choosing this option, you gain access to expert advice from the

Below: Designed by Robin Day in 1953 for S. Hille & Co., the 'Q Stak' chair is typical of its era in terms of the bent laminated plywood seat and its tubular steel legs. Its cherry wood veneer adds warmth to the simple form.

auctioneers, who can help you to establish the value of a piece. A further advantage, if the auction house has a website, is that your lots will be listed online and therefore have the potential to be seen by many more people. Any listing in the catalogue, online, or otherwise, will include a brief description of the piece, along with an estimate of the price to act as a guide when bidding. To some extent you can determine the price of the piece – it helps to look at back catalogues and reputable price guides for a ballpark figure – but the final decision rests with the auctioneers. In all other instances, and unless otherwise professionally advised, discuss setting a reserve on your item. This means that if the highest bid is lower than your reserve, the sale will not go through.

When selling at auction, you must always account for the fact that the auction house will charge a seller's premium on any goods you sell, which usually amounts to 15–20 per cent, which they will deduct from the "hammer price". A further disadvantage of selling at auction is that if your piece does not sell you have to think of an alternative strategy.

SELLING THROUGH A DEALER

You could try selling a piece to an antique dealer at his own establishment. It may be that you buy regularly from one or two dealers and have a good relationship with them. Many dealers will buy pieces, as long as they like them and are satisfied that they are in a good enough condition to sell. A dealer will have to consider potential restoration costs (if any are necessary) and collection and delivery costs (if relevant) among other things when coming up with a price for your goods, and you cannot always expect to make money on the deal. This is, of course, subject to how long you have had a piece, when and where you bought it, whether its value has increased substantially since that time, and how you have looked after it. Fashions change and you may find your antiques are worth more or less as a result.

Another selling option through an antique dealer is for him or her to take a piece on a sale or return (SOR) basis. Many dealers are happy to do this,

Above: Decorative household objects from jardinières to odd plates, picture frames, silver-plated gravy boats and glass vases try to find new homes at a fair. Always decide what you would like in advance, and label each item with its price clearly displayed.

particularly if you bought the piece from them originally or if it is something with which they are particularly associated. Again, the dealer will have to consider the cost implications (making a profit to cover their overheads, potential bank charges, possible restoration needs, delivery charges, and so on), which means you might be offered less than you paid for the piece.

SELLING AT A TRADE FAIR

There is no reason why you cannot try to sell antiques at a trade fair, and there are a couple of options open to you. First, you can attend the fair just as you would when buying – on the days that the event is open to the public. If you are familiar with the fair, you will know roughly which dealers to approach with specific items. The alternative, which is really only worth doing if you have a good number of items to sell, is to take a pitch at the fair yourself (though this is not always possible so check with the organisers first). The fair websites have all the relevant information on how to do this and the fee is obviously higher than attending as a regular buyer. Be aware, however, that pitches are usually reserved for frequent attendees, and any spares may be awarded on a first-come, first-served basis. There may even be a waiting list. Should you be lucky, however, the advantage of doing this is that you become a trader yourself and can show your wares to many more dealers than you would otherwise manage. Another benefit is that whatever you sell gets taken away immediately and is paid for in cash. If items are too large or delicate to take to the fair, make sure that you have a good supply of photographs, with the items pictured clearly against a plain background, along with details of dimensions and any damage or markings.

Above: *When selling online, be sure to include any details relating to the history or provenance of an item. This Chinese Kangxi period vase and cover, made c1690-1700, is made more desirable as it came from the salvaged cargo of the Vung Tau shipwreck. It should bear labels from the 1992 Christie's auction to prove this fact.*

SELLING ONLINE

You can, of course, sell online. In fact, selling through sites such as eBay is quite a good way to get started, beginning with low-value items until you get a feel for it. You do not have to make any special journeys to auction houses or approach dealers in their shops or at fairs. Depending on what you are selling, the most you will have to do is package the goods and get them to a post office. (You can sell large items as "buyer collect", although this will narrow your field.)

Also, by putting your wares on eBay, you guarantee that many hundreds of people across the world will see your lot, including avid collectors, auctioneers, and dealers, all of whom use the site regularly.

You need to register with eBay, and you will be charged a nominal fee for each item you sell. There are various methods of selling in addition to the standard auction system, such as "Buy it Now" or "Make me an Offer", but you will be charged extra for these services.

If selling on eBay, make sure that your description is as accurate as possible, and always supply a number of good photographs that show the piece off at its best. Do not try to hide undesirable scratches or watermarks, but make them known from the outset. Be prepared to answer questions helpfully (and promptly) and always put a true cost for postage and packing in your listing. There is more information on eBay's website, which is well presented and easily negotiated.

DECIDING TO SELL

Whether or not to sell an item is always the trickiest question, and only you will know if you are emotionally ready to part with something. But there are other considerations. In particular, is it a good time to sell? All antiques go in and out of fashion – some have longer spells, while others reach unprecedented values for a short time only. In deciding whether this is a good time to sell, you must first gauge the market.

Below: You will have the best chance of obtaining the best price if the piece you are selling is clean and looks inviting and appealing. The early 20th century French Louis XV–style bergère below is an excellent example – it has been cleaned, waxed and polished.

Given that you will have done some research when buying a piece and will know whether or not you paid the going rate, the first thing you could do is find out whether it has held its value or not. Ask around – dealers and auction houses usually offer fair advice in these matters. And refer to reputable price guides and websites for further information you can trust.

If it is some time since you bought the piece, spend some time brushing up on what you know about it. All potential buyers will have questions for you – how long have you had the piece, does it have any provenance, what date is it, is there any damage, and so on – and you must be well versed in giving the right answers. It is also important that your piece is in the best condition that it could be. This does not mean that you should be scrubbing away at awkward stains or patching up bits of chipped veneer. You must take exceptional care in doing anything, as many attempts at increasing the value of a piece actually result in devaluing it unwittingly. If in doubt, find out how best to care for and repair the items you have. Being in good condition makes them instantly more attractive to the buyer. This is particularly true of auction houses (because a better condition means higher bids) and dealers (because less work means more profit and a quicker sale).

Try to get an idea of the price a given item goes for – you can check back catalogues of auction houses, auction websites, dealer websites, and so on. Decide on a price that you want for your piece and then think about the highest discount you would be prepared to give. If someone offers less than your discounted price, do not feel obliged to take it. Just try elsewhere.

RESOURCES

There is an enormous variety of information available. Choose the source you like best, but here are details of some of the best-known:

WEBSITES

BBC Homes & Antiques magazine
www.bbchomesandantiques.com
Information about BBC antiques programmes including 'Cracking Antiques' and 'Antiques Roadshow'. Find out when programmes are due to be broadcast, how to take part in the shows and look behind the scenes. .

Miller's Antiques & Collectables
www.millersonline.com
Includes a catalogue of authenticated antiques and collectables, articles, a fully illustrated A-Z of terms, a dealer, appraiser and auctioneer database, a guide to silver hallmarks; and information about care and repair.

Live Auctioneers
www.liveauctioneers.com
Allows users to search catalogues from selected auction houses in Europe, the USA and the United Kingdom. Visitors to the site can bid live via the Internet into salerooms as auctions happen. Registered users can also access past catalogues.

The Saleroom.com
www.the-saleroom.com
Allows users to search catalogues from selected auction houses in Europe, the USA and the United Kingdom. Visitors to the site can bid live via the internet into salerooms as auctions happen. Registered users can also search through an archive of past catalogues.

eBay *www.ebay.com*
Undoubtedly the largest and most diverse of the online auction sites, allowing users to buy and sell in an online marketplace with over 100 million registered users from across the world.

ArtFact *www.artfact.com*
A comprehensive database of worldwide auction listings from over 2,000 art, antiques and collectables auction houses. Search sales and find information on collectors' fields. Online bidding live into auctions as they happen is also offered.

The Antiques Trade Gazette
www.antiquestradegazette.com
The online edition of the UK trade newspaper, including auction and fair listings, informative auction sale reviews, news and events.

Maine Antique Digest
www.maineantiquedigest.com
Online version of America's trade newspaper including news, articles, fair and auction listings.

La Gazette du Drouot *www.drouot.com*
The online home of the magazine listing all auctions to be held in France at the Hotel de Drouot in Paris. An online subscription enables you to download the magazine online.

Auction.fr *www.auction.fr*
An online database of auctions at French auction houses. A subscription allows users to search past catalogues and prices realized.

Go Antiques/Worthpoint *www.goantiques.com* and *www.worthpoint.com*
An online global aggregator for art, antiques and collectables dealers. Dealers' stock is showcased online, with users able to browse and buy.

FAIR AND SHOW ORGANIZERS

IACF (International Antiques & Collectors Fair)
Newark (Notts), Ardingly (Sussex), Detling (Kent), Swinderby (Nr. Lincoln) and Shepton Mallet (Somerset). *www.iacf.co.uk*

Clarion Events, Antiques for Everyone
Birmingham. www.antiquesforeveryone.co.uk
Olympia Antiques Fairs, London.
www.olympia-antiques.co.uk

Nelson Fairs, Alexandra Palace, London.
www.nelsonfairs.com

Arthur Swallow Fairs, Lincoln Showground, Lincolnshire., *www.arthurswallowfairs.co.uk*

Penman Fairs, Vetted antiques and fine art fairs in Chelsea (London), Chester (Cheshire), Kensington (London), Petersfield (Hampshire), Towcester (Northamptonshire), and West London. *www.penman-fairs.co.uk*

NATIONAL AND INTERNATIONAL ANTIQUES ORGANIZATIONS

BADA: British Antique Dealers' Association
Trade association for the leading antique dealers in Britain. Members adhere to a strict code of practice and safeguards are provided, including independent arbitration if disputes arise. Holds annual fairs. *www.bada.org*

LAPADA: The Association of Art and Antique Dealers , The largest association of professional art and antiques dealers in the UK. Membership is open to those who meet the Association's requirements as to experience, quality of stock and knowledge of their subject. Holds annual fairs., *www.lapada.org*

CINOA, Non-profit international federation of associations for antique and art dealers. Membership is open to associations that bind their dealer members to reputable standards of quality and expertise., *www.cinoa.org*

REGIONAL ANTIQUES ORGANIZATIONS

BABAADA: Bath & Bradford on Avon Antique Dealers Association, *www.babaada.com and www.bath.co.uk/babaada/babaada.asp*

Cotswold Antiques Dealers Association
www.cotswolds-antiques-art.com

Thames Valley Antiques Dealers Association *www.tvada.co.uk*

Kensington Church Street Antique Dealers Association, *www.antiques-london.com*

West of England Antique Dealers' Association *www.weada.co.uk*

Portobello Antique Dealers Association
www.portobelloroad.co.uk

Irish Antique Dealers Association
www.iada.ie

UNDERSTANDING HALLMARKS

Since ancient times, silver and gold have been of great commercial importance. As a result, it became necessary to create a standard of purity to which everyone must adhere. In England in 1300, a lion's head mark was introduced. Known at the time as a 'leopart', it has evolved into the leopard's head mark that is used today. The crown was removed c1821-22. In 1327, a charter empowered the Goldsmith's Company at Goldsmith's Hall in London to test and mark, or 'assay', silver, resulting in the term 'hallmark'. Since then other assay offices have appeared. Look at specialist silver & silver plate marks reference books to interpret hallmarks. All British silver, with few exceptions, is hallmarked. There are usually four symbols, which may be found in any order. Each has its own meaning. From left:

- The maker's mark of the silversmith.
- The 'lion passant',
- The standard purity mark.
- The assay office mark .

The date letter, indicating the year a piece was marked (and most probably made). The shape and style indicates a particular year. If a piece of silver does not have the complete set of four marks it is likely that it is from another country or a piece of silver plate bearing a hallmark-style trademark.

Other marks may also appear in addition to these four. From 1784-1890, a tax was imposed on silver and to prove the tax had been paid, a fifth mark of the sovereign's head in profile was added. For the first six months of 1785, this was

Above: A typical hallmark showing, from left: the maker's mark; the lion passant; the standard purity mark; the date letter. This mark is for London, 1905.

intaglio (fully indented), but after this period, it became cameo (raised), like other marks. A mark showing George III (near right) was used from mid 1785 until 1820. Another showing Queen Victoria (far right) was used from 1837 until 1890 when the tax was finally abolished.

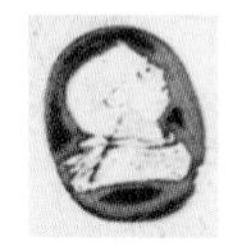

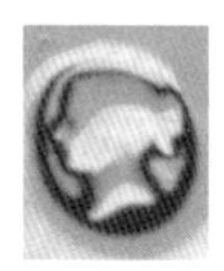

OTHER MARKS

From 1697-1720, the silver standard was raised and 'Britannia' marks were used. Other marks showing the sovereign's head in profile indicate years of production: George V's silver jubilee 1934-35, Elizabeth II's coronation 1953, and silver jubilee 1977. From 1976, some assay offices in certain countries used a control mark which became legally acceptable internationally.

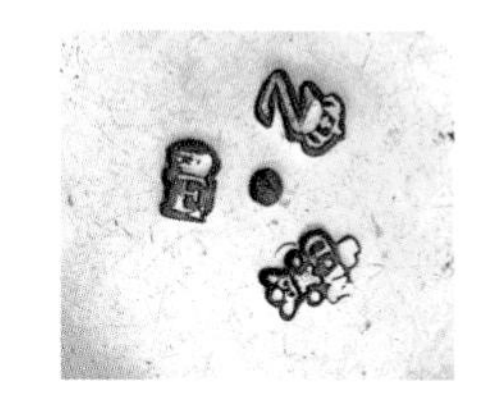

SILVER IMPORTED INTO BRITAIN

From 1904 all silver imported into the UK had to be marked with its purity, eg; '.925' (top centre right). In 1973, the decimal point was removed. In addition, a date letter was applied and each UK assay office had its own mark.

OTHER EUROPEAN SILVER MARKS

Top left: The fifth tax related hallmark, of George III, used from 1785–1820.

Top right: The fifth tax–related hallmark, of Queen Victoria, used from 1837–90.

Top centre: An example of marks used on silver imported into Britain from 1904.

Bottom centre: An example of French hallmarks.

Bottom: A silver mark for Danish maker Georg Jensen.

In general, marking systems used by European countries were inconsistent, if they existed at all. Many marks are of little use, but city or country marks may be more reliable. Some of the many examples are shown below.

FRENCH & OTHER HALLMARKS

Marks were used as early as 1272, but the system was inconsistent. In general, before the French Revolution in 1789, up to four marks were used. These comprise a maker's mark, a community or 'juranada' mark, a city charge mark and sometimes a related city discharge mark.

The word 'STERLING' in capital letters generally indicates that a silver object was made in the US. However, not all pieces bear this word, and other marks are known. Many pieces are simply marked with a maker's mark. Unlike the UK, the name often appears in full within a border, rather than as initials. A symbol may also be used, such as the knight on horseback mark, which was the symbol for Mary C. Knight, or the capital 'S' in a shield symbol, which was used by Simons Bros.

CERAMIC MARKS

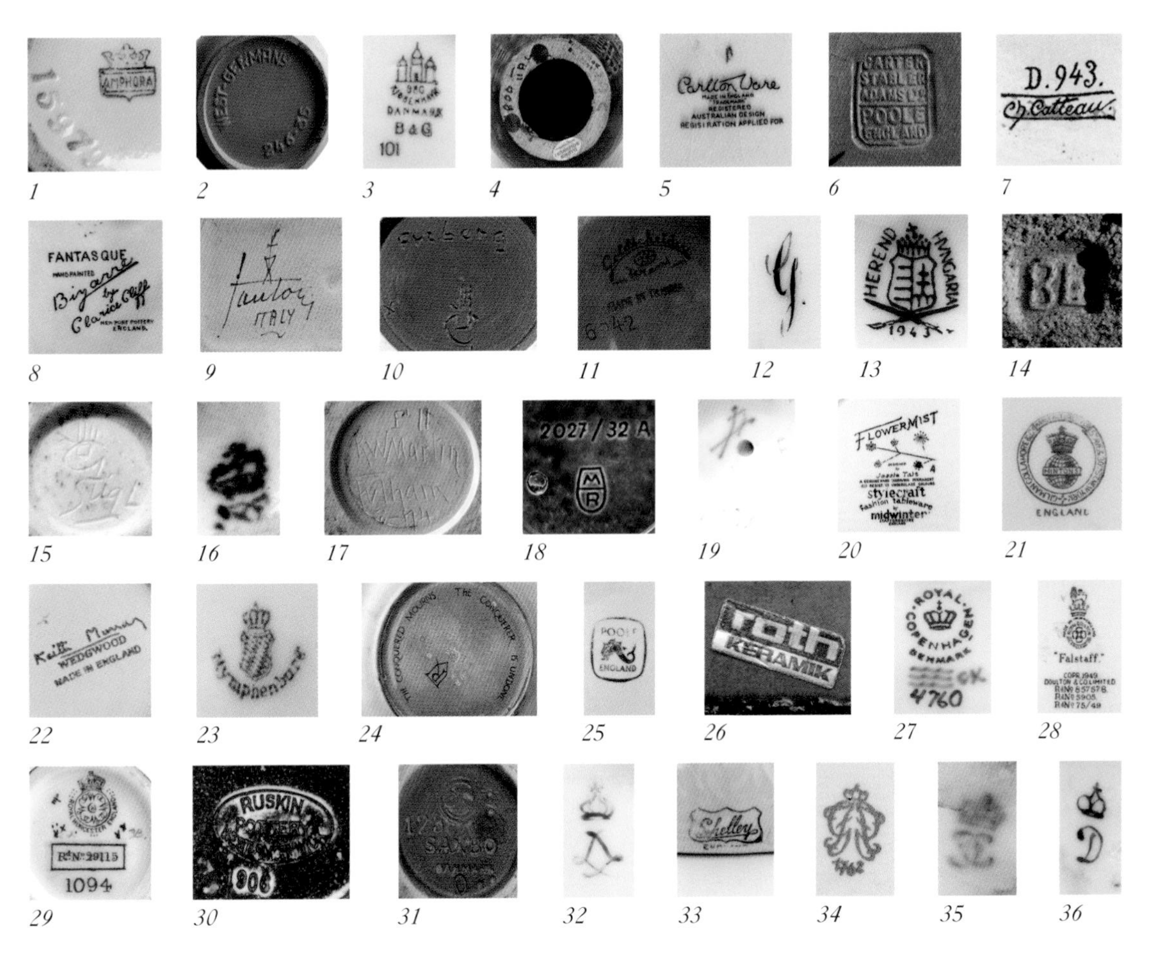

1. *Amphora Bohemia (now Czech Republic) late19th-early 20thC* **2.** *Bay, West German 1950s-1970s* **3.** *Bing & Grondhal Denmark 20thC* **4.** *Bitossi, Italy, c1960* **5.** *Carlton ware, UK, 1930s* **6.** *Poole, UK, c1930* **7.** *Charles Catteau for Boch Freres, Belgium c1925* **8.** *Clarice Cliff, UK, 1930s* **9.** *Fantoni, Italy, 1950s-70s* **10.** *Gustavsberg, Berndt Friberg, Sweden 1950s-60s* **11.** *Goldscheider, Austria, c1925* **12.** *Gotha Germany 1802-34* **13.** *Herend Hungary 20thC* **14.** *Bernard Leach, UK, 1930s-72* **15.** *Gustavsberg, Stig Lindberg, Sweden 1950s-70s* **16.** *Ludwigsburg Germany 1758-93* **17.** *Martin Brothers, UK, late 19thC* **18.** *Marzi & Remy, West Germany, 1950s-60s* **19.** *Meissen, Germany,* **20.** *Midwinter, UK, c1960* **21.** *Minton, UK, c1873-1912* **22.** *Keith Murray for Wedgwood, UK, 1930s* **23.** *Nymphenburg Germany, 20thC* **24.** *Pilkington's Royal Lancastrian UK 1903-13* **25.** *Poole, UK, mid–late 20thC* **26.** *Roth, West Germany, 1970s* **27.** *Royal Copenhagen, Denmark, 20thC* **28.** *Royal Doulton, UK, 20thC* **29.** *Royal Worcester, UK, late 19thC* **30.** *Ruskin Pottery UK c1900–1933* **31.** *Saxbo, Denmark, 1950s–60s* **32.** *Sevres, France, c1770* **33.** *Shelley, UK, c1930* **34. Volk** **35.** *Wallendrorf, Germany, early 20thC* **36.** *Wolfsohn, Helena Germany 19thC*

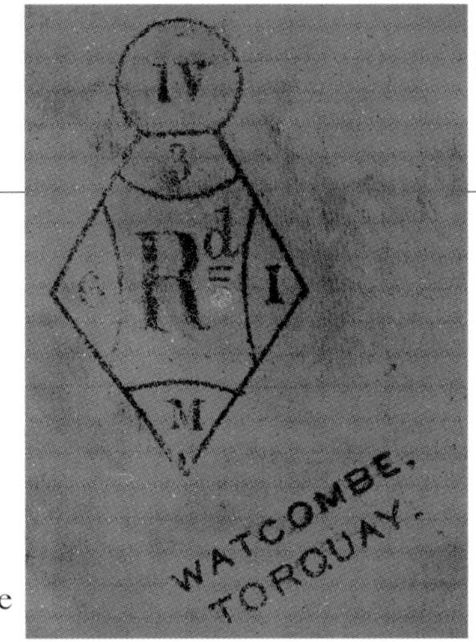

DESIGN REGISTRATION MARKS

One of the most useful marks for dating is the Design Registration mark. Registration began in 1839 following the Copyright of Design Act. The insignia (diamond-shaped mark) was used from 1842. The insignia also showed what material the item was made from (its class) and how many items were included (bundle or package). The Rd in the centre of the diamond stands for registered design.

YEAR

The letters were not used in sequence but as follows: 1842-1867 (features a number in the right hand corner of the diamond)

A – 1845	E – 1855	I – 1846	M – 1859	Q – 1866	U – 1848	Y – 1853
B – 1858	F – 1847	J – 1854	N – 1864	R – 1861	V – 1850	Z – 1860
C – 1844	G – 1863	K – 1857	O – 1862	S – 1849	W – 1865	
D – 1852	H – 1843	L – 1856	P – 1851	T – 1867	X – 1842	

1868-1883 (letter in the right hand corner of the diamond)

A – 1871	E – 1881	I – 1872	L – 1882	U – 1874	Y – 1879
C – 1870	F – 1873	J – 1880	P – 1877	V – 1876	
D – 1878	H – 1869	K – 1883	S – 1875	X – 1868	

The exceptions to these are: in 1857 the letter R was used from 1-19 September. In 1860 the letter K was used for December. From 1-6 March 1878, W was used for the year in place of D, and G was used for the month in place of W.

MONTHS

The months from both periods are shown as follows:

A – December	D – September	H – April	M – June
B – October	E – May	I – July	R – August
C/O – January	G – February	K – November	W – March

CLASS

Sometimes the clerks mis-classified items so it is possible to find a bookbinding misfiled as a carpet.

Class 1 - Metal	Class 7 - Printed Shawls	Class 12 (ii) - Other Fabrics (Damasks)
Class 2 - Wood	Class 8 - Other Shawls	Class 13 – Lace
Class 3 - Glass	Class 9 - Yarn	
Class 4 - Earthenware	Class 10 - Printed Fabrics	
Class 5 - Paper Hangings	Class 11 - Furnitures (printed fabrics)	
Class 6 - Carpets	Class 12 (i) - Other Fabrics	

REGISTERED NUMBER

A series of consecutive numbers were used from 1884, nearly always prefixed by Rd or Rd No (Registered or Registered Number). This guide, showing the number reached on 1st January each year is an estimate only: The system is still in use today.

1: 1884	141273: 1890	268393: 1896	385500: 1902	519000: 1908	895,000: 1960
19754: 1885	163767: 1891	291241: 1897	402500: 1903	550000: 1909	944,932: 1970
40480: 1886	185713: 1892	311658: 1898	420000: 1904	673,750: 1920	993,012: 1980
64520: 1887	205240: 1893	331707: 1899	447000: 1905	751,160: 1930	2,007,720: 1990
90483: 1888	224720: 1894	351202: 1900	471000: 1906	837,520: 1940	2,089,190: 2000
116648: 1889	246975: 1895	368154: 1901	494000: 1907	860,854: 1950	

FURNITURE CONSTRUCTION

Tilt-top table

Drop-leaf table

George I side chair c1720

Rococo-style wing chair c1900

George III dining chair c1790

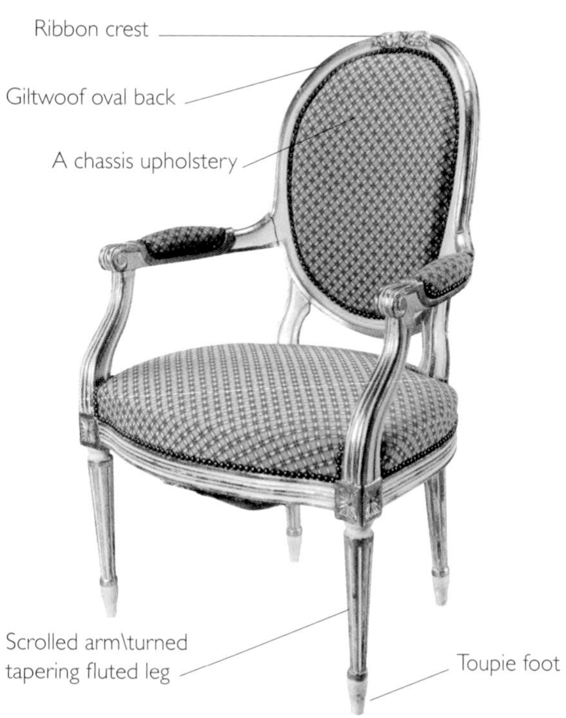

Louis XVI-style armchair c1900

INDEX

ACKNOWEDGEMENTS & THANKS

Mark & Kathryn would like to thank everyone at Silver River, especially Amanda, Donna, Daisy and Dan for being clever and masterminding the whole thing. Also thanks to Simon for safe driving, cheerful conversation and marshmallows; to Ami, Sam and Kate for being so organised and for making sure we always got there safely and on time; to Carrie & Chrissie for being so bloomin' good with cushions and so much more; and to Chris, Christopher, Adam and all the lovely sound men and editors for making us look and sound so good (hopefully).

Big thanks to the visionary team at BBC2; Alex Menzies, Janice Hadlow and Jo Ball. Without you none of this would have happened!

Heartfelt thanks to the other two Jo's in our lives – Wander and Brooks, for being showbiz mums. Thanks also to David, Tracey, Yasia, Pene, Julie, Anna, Caroline, Peter and Carolin and the team at Mitchell Beazley for producing this tremendous tome.

We'd also like to thank our contributors, Dean and Ellen, Rebecca, David and Charlotte, Roy and Katy, Jody and Adrian, and Karen for making us many cups of tea and letting us loose on their homes.

We're also grateful to the following dealers and fair organisers who helped us: Tony Bush of Bushwood Antiques near Hemel Hempstead, Suzanna at Three Angels in Brighton, Catherine Shinn of Decorative Textiles in Cheltenham, Benjamin at Junk Deluxe in Margate, Franco at Salvatore Antiques in Bolton, Rupert at the Leominster Reclamation & Architectural Salvage, and every one at the International Antiques & Collectors' Fairs at Shepton Mallet and Ardingly, The French Depot in Bexhill, Arthur Swallow Fairs, Top Banana Antiques Mall in Tetbury, the Hemswell Antiques Centres near Lincoln, Bygone Times in Eccleston, the Crystal Palace Antiques Warehouse and at The Antiques & Secondhand Warehouse in Leominster. And thanks to Barry, who was always cheerful when the golf buggies arrived.

Mark would like to thank Beth & Beverley Adams and Ian Broughton of Alfie's Antiques Market, Dr. Graham Cooley, Fergus Gambon of Bonhams, Kevin & Ina Harris of Undercurrents, Jeanette Hayhurst, Stewart Hofgartner of Below Stairs, Andy McConnell of Glass etc, Judith Miller of Miller's, Steven Moore of Anderson & Garland, Gillian Neale, Simon Shaw & Lloyd Farmar, and his marvellous parents, for their support, expert advice and sage words. As ever, I couldn't have done it without Philip.

Kathryn would like to thank the lovely Mags for being her body double when things got tough, and Margaret for being a fairy godmother. Big shout out to Sarah Arnett for her beautiful frocks and Tina Lillienthal for her bonkers jeweller. Tremendous thanks to the crack team of grandparents who child wrangled unstintingly, to Rox and Stan for general cuteness, and to my lovely, lovely husband Simon who was a single dad for months on end without complaining (much) but was just very proud…

Dotted throughout the book are images from the rooms featured in the television series that accompanies this book. Here are the details if you want to look them up:

Chelmsford: 9 (top left); 36; 83; 14; 182
Fleet: 5 (right); 9 (bottom right); 77; 204; 205 (left)
Hereford: 5 (left); 9 (bottom left); 30; 74; 90
Lincoln: 2; 3; 211
Newark: 9 (top right); 20; 34; 56; 205 (bottom)
Stockport: 7; 10-11; 27; 71